by
Gregory Crafts

STEELE SPRING
STAGE RIGHTS

www.stagerights.com

For all stage performance inquiries, please contact:

Steele Spring Stage Rights
3845 Cazador Street
Los Angeles, CA 90065
(323) 739-0413
www.stagerights.com

CHARACTERS

GARRETT - The Geek, 17

Garrett is an outsider with a secret. Constantly tortured in school and relegated to the social fringe, he just tries to get through each day as best as possible. The only bright spots in his life are his two friends, Bryan and Diz, and the place they all share: a wondrous game world called Haven. All of this changes, however, when he's noticed by the most popular cheerleader in school. Suddenly, things start to look up! He's in love, finding confidence and enjoying his daily life for the first time... until the past comes back to haunt him. Harassed by Nicole's angry ex-boyfriend, and forced to deal with his best friend Diz's jealousy and suspicion, Garrett's life will never be the same.

NICOLE - The Cheerleader, 16

With wisdom and maturity well beyond her years, Nicole is far from your typical cheerleader. She dumps Jesse after discovering him cheating on her. From there, she meets Garrett and is immediately smitten by his sincerity and charming awkwardness. She delves deeper and deeper into Garrett's world, thrilling him, but also inciting an aggressive Jesse and jealous Diz to act against her.

BRYAN - The Social Butterfly, 16

Bryan is a dichotomy. Part Super Jock, part Über Geek. He splits his weekends between wrestling practice with Jesse and going to Haven with Garrett and Diz. Genuine and good-natured, he manages to walk a fine line and fit in with even the most extreme social categories. When things start to change, however, he's forced to pick a side. Little does he know, that decision will affect his life forever.

CHARACTERS (CONT'D)

DIZ - The Freak, 15
Clad in an oversized hoodie, baggy jeans and a moniker borrowed from her favorite Tiny Toon, Danielle Watts may as well be just one of the guys. Garrett's best friend and confidant, she secretly harbors a fierce crush on him but doesn't know how to express it. When Garrett starts dating Nicole, Diz's jealousy threatens to get the better of her, and drive her to unspeakable lengths to win him back.

JESSE - The Jock, 17
Alpha male through-and-through, Jesse is a typical swaggering high school jock. His life is turned upside down, however, when his girlfriend Nicole discovers him having sex with her best friend. Furthering his disgrace, Nicole starts dating Garrett, the biggest geek in the school and Jesse's usual target for abuse. Fueled by rage and humiliation, Jesse will stop at nothing to take back what he sees as rightfully his.

Note: Bryan and Jesse also double as Shadows in Act II Scene IV. Also, it is recommended that the Reporters, Student and various voices are done as pre-recorded sound cues.

TIME & PLACE

Post-Columbine Suburbia, USA

SETTING

This play takes place in more than half a dozen different locations with several quick changes. This show can be done with a set as simple as a table and three folding chairs arranged in different configurations to represent each place. A projector can be integrated into the production to accent each location and provide a richer backdrop. Transitions between scenes should be fast, but it is suggested that clips of music are used to help bridge scenes together. The story is set a year after the Columbine Massacre. It is suggested that any music used should be from no later than 2001.

RUN TIME

2 Acts, 90-105 Minutes

PRODUCTION HISTORY

Originally Produced in 2009 by Theatre Unleashed at The Sherry Theatre in North Hollywood, CA.

For Vance

PROLOGUE

A projector screen hangs as the backdrop to a bare stage. The show begins in blackout. Speakers crackle to life as short series of pre-recorded news segments play in the darkness.

REPORTER #1: Another tragic school shooting rocked the nation today. Barely a year after the massacre at Columbine High School in Littleton, Colorado, the bodies of almost a dozen students and faculty from our own Piedmont High School were removed after a brutal rampage that was over before many knew anything had happ—

REPORTER #2: —he shooting began in the hallways where the gunman opened fire on a crowd of students, then moved into one of the athletic roo—

REPORTER #3: —arrett Lang, 17, a sophomore at Piedmont. Friends say he was the quiet type an—

REPORTER #4: —wearing a long, black trench coat, a signature for this kind of violence, and armed with multiple handguns. The thoughts and prayers of everyone here at Channel 7 go out to the members of the Piedmont High School community and especially the families of the vict—

STUDENT: —ll of a sudden, I heard something like firecrackers going off, then people were running and screaming—

REPORTER #2: —said they never saw it comi—

REPORTER #1: —nother tragic incident of teen violence leaving a community reeling and families asking, "why?" Will we ever know the answer?

The news broadcast is consumed in a burst of static, then fades out. The words "3 Months Earlier" flash across the projection screen.

ACT I

SCENE 1

THE HAVEN CAMPGROUNDS

GARRETT, DIZ and BRYAN enter, all decked out in a mish-mash of homemade medieval-style costumes and sports pads.

DIZ: Another job well done.

GARRETT: Indeed, Lady Mortania. Never again will the lands of Haven be threatened by the dark magic of the evil Lord Malkor. The forces of good have reigned supre—

BRYAN *(interjecting)*: Dude.

GARRETT: What is this "dude" you speak of, good Sir Sway?

BRYAN: Garrett, game's over.

GARRETT: It's Ivan.

BRYAN: Garrett, the game ended an hour ago. So, save the in-character grandstanding for next month.

GARRETT: But I'm in the moment.

BRYAN: You're the only one.

GARRETT: Bryan, why do you always need to piss in my Frosted Flakes?

BRYAN: I'm not. I'm just ready to go back.

DIZ: Why?

BRYAN: Because after a weekend of running around the woods in hockey pads and rubber ears, beating people with foam swords all night long, I'm ready for a shower and a hot meal.

DIZ: Pussy.

BRYAN: Well, you are what you—

GARRETT *(interjecting)*: Please. Come up with something original.

DIZ: Seriously. Why would you ever want to leave?

BRYAN: Because this is a game. I already have a life.

GARRETT: That makes one of us.

BRYAN: Don't start.

GARRETT: I'm not. I'm just saying that if I could, I'd be here all the time.

BRYAN: Please. Next, you'll say you wish it was real.

GARRETT: I do.

DIZ: Me too.

BRYAN: Remind me why I like to hang out with you guys again?

DIZ: Because you like everybody.

GARRETT: And you're almost as geeky as we are.

BRYAN: I wouldn't go that far.

GARRETT: So, you're both going to be at the event next month, right?

BRYAN: If I don't have a wrestling tournament.

GARRETT: Ah, off competing with the brute squad.

DIZ: He's on the Brute Squad.

GARRETT: He is the Brute Squad.

BRYAN: Geeks.

SCENE 2

A HOUSE PARTY

Same night. NICOLE enters and moves to the center of the party to address a large crowd of her peers.

NICOLE: Attention everyone. I have an announcement to make. Thank you. My boyfriend, Jesse, Mr. Captain of the Varsity Wrestling Team, Mr. "God's Gift to Women," self-proclaimed, of course, is now single. That's right, folks, he's back on the market!

JESSE enters. NICOLE doesn't notice him.

I know this may come as a shock to some, but, believe me, it's for the best. Ladies, he's available immediately for your dating pleasure. He's not much for conversation, unless you like endless prattling on about football and "that time he pinned that kid from O'Connell in the State Finals," but he tries hard. Yes, he may be lacking in intelligence and sensitivity, as well as other "significant" areas, but he's not that bad, really. Anyone want his number? It'll be up on the bathroom wall later under the heading "For a good time, call Meathead."

JESSE: Nikki, what's going on?

NICOLE: It's Nicole now, douche bag, and I could have asked you the same thing but it was pretty obvious. Let me spell it out for you— we're over.

JESSE: What? Why?

NICOLE: Thank you for your attention, everyone! Party on. Party on.

NICOLE turns to leave but JESSE grabs her and spins her around.

JESSE: Now you just wait a min—

NICOLE slaps JESSE across the face. All conversation and party noise stops.

NICOLE: Don't you ever touch me again.

> *NICOLE turns back around and leaves JESSE stunned in the middle of the party. He comes to his senses.*

JESSE: What are you lookin' at?

> *JESSE turns and exits.*

SCENE 3

THE WRESTLING ROOM

> *BRYAN and JESSE are practicing their wrestling techniques. Jesse is recapping his version of the party.*

JESSE: Yeah, that bitch was getting stale. I kicked her to the curb Saturday night.

BRYAN: So, she dumped you.

JESSE: I just said I dumped her.

BRYAN: No need to save face, dude. It's all over the school. I wasn't even at the party Saturday night and I heard about it.

JESSE: Yeah, where were you? It was a great party.

BRYAN: ...Camping.

JESSE: Really.

BRYAN: Yeah, with my old man. It's a tradition.

JESSE: Sounds gay.

BRYAN: Whatever.

JESSE: You guys got back late. You missed church on Sunday.

> *GARRETT and DIZ knock on the door to the wrestling room. They're both in black heavy metal t-shirts, baggy black pants and black combat boots. Garrett wears a long black trench coat over his clothes and Diz sports a spiked collar and matching black studded leather cuff. Garrett carries a black notebook tucked under his arm.*

What do you want, faggot?

GARRETT: Hey Bryan, we've got your part of the treas— stuff... from this weekend. It's in my locker.

BRYAN: Not now, Garrett.

GARRETT: It's ok, just find me after practice.

BRYAN: Whatever. I gotta get back before Coach flips.

GARRETT: No worries.

GARRETT and DIZ exit.

JESSE: Camping, huh?

SCENE 4

INSIDE THE CAFETERIA

GARRETT is sitting alone at a cafeteria table. He's absentmindedly shuffling a deck of game cards while reading from his notebook. NICOLE enters, wearing her cheerleading outfit, and approaches his table. Garrett doesn't notice.

NICOLE: Hi.

GARRETT: What?

NICOLE: Hi.

GARRETT looks around. She must be talking to him.

GARRETT: The pep rally's in the gym.

NICOLE: Huh?

GARRETT: You're a cheerleader.

NICOLE: Yeah.

GARRETT: I'm a freak.

NICOLE: Ok.

GARRETT: I'm sure this is a violation of the Natural Order of the Universe.

NICOLE: I don't understand.

GARRETT: Never mind. Forgive me if this is obvious, but... why are you talking to me?

NICOLE: What?

GARRETT: Seriously, if this is some prank or something, you're wasting your time.

NICOLE: Why would you think that?

GARRETT: Because you're talking to me. Cheerleaders don't talk to people like me.

NICOLE: Have you thought about looking beyond the uniform?

GARRETT: Why should I? You guys don't.

NICOLE: We don't?

GARRETT: No.

NICOLE: If that's true, why am I still here talking to you, then?

GARRETT: I think I asked you that.

NICOLE: You did.

GARRETT: Well, if I did, that means I've got no idea.

NICOLE: I'm curious about your cards.

GARRETT: Oh.

NICOLE: What are they?

GARRETT: They're for a game.

> GARRETT closes his black notebook and puts his decks away. NICOLE sits down across from him.

NICOLE: What kind of game?

GARRETT: It's called Magic.

NICOLE: I think my little brother plays.

GARRETT: How old is your brother?

NICOLE: Seven.

GARRETT: He plays Pokémon.

NICOLE: That's the one.

GARRETT: This is not Pokémon.

NICOLE: Ok. So, how do you play this game?

GARRETT: Do you really want to know?

NICOLE: Yeah.

GARRETT: It's geek stuff.

NICOLE: Don't judge. I'm interested. I see you guys playing here all the time.

> Beat. GARRETT withdraws two playing decks from his bag.

GARRETT: Ok. Well, here, take one of my decks and shuffle it up.

NICOLE: What do the different colors mean?

GARRETT: I'll get to that in a second. First—

> JESSE enters. He sees NICOLE and heads over to her.

JESSE: Hey. What's going on?

NICOLE: Nothing.

JESSE: Nothing? What the fuck is this? Don't tell me you're getting into this shit.

GARRETT: Dude, it's just a game.

JESSE: Nobody asked you, faggot. You'll shut the fuck up and stay away from my girl if you know what's good for you.

GARRETT: Hey dude, she ca—

NICOLE: Your girl? I dumped you last week. If you forgot, you can ask anyone at Sarah's party. I'm sure they'll remind you. They all saw it happen...

GARRETT: Y'know, if you guys need to talk in private, I can go.

JESSE *(to Garrett)*: Shut up. *(to Nicole)* Whatever. You'll be back.

NICOLE: Right. Just keep telling yourself that.

JESSE: You'll see.

JESSE exits.

GARRETT: What a dick.

NICOLE: Yeah, no kidding.

GARRETT: Wonder what his problem is.

NICOLE: I dumped him.

GARRETT: Oh, yeah. Well, that would be a problem.

NICOLE: Mmm hmm.

GARRETT: Why?

NICOLE: Walked in on him having sex with my best friend. Ex-best friend.

GARRETT: And that would be grounds for dumping.

Beat. GARRETT starts shuffling his decks.

NICOLE: I'm Nicole.

GARRETT: I know. We had History together last year.

NICOLE: We did?

GARRETT: Yeah. I let you copy my homework.

NICOLE: Oh, I don't remember.

GARRETT: You copied it every day for the semester.

NICOLE: Wow, um, thanks again.

GARRETT: Think nothing of it. Again.

NICOLE: Yeah. So...

GARRETT: What?

NICOLE: What's your name?

GARRETT: Garrett.

NICOLE: Yeah. So, Garrett, you want to go catch a movie?

GARRETT: What?

NICOLE *(slowly)*: Do you want to go see a movie with me?

GARRETT: Uh... sure.

NICOLE: Ok, don't get so excited.

GARRETT: No, I'm not, I mean, I am. Excited, that is. I'm just surprised, too.

NICOLE: Surprised? Why?

GARRETT: Cheerleader. Freak. Violation of Natural Order.

NICOLE: Whatever! We can go see a movie. I mean, it's not like it's going to be a date or anything.

GARRETT: It's not? *(beat)* Oh, ok.

NICOLE: I just want to hang out and do something tonight. It's Friday after all.

GARRETT: Ok.

NICOLE: So... meet me at 8?

GARRETT: Sounds good.

NICOLE: Oh, and bring your cards. I still want you to teach me.

GARRETT: Seriously?

NICOLE: Seriously.

GARRETT: Ok.

> *Beat. NICOLE starts to leave. GARRETT thinks she's out of earshot.*

Holy shit.

NICOLE: What?

GARRETT: Nothing. Nothing. I'm just... wow. Yeah. Uh, I'll see you tonight! 8 o'clock, right?

NICOLE: Yeah.

GARRETT: Cool. Ok. Wow. *(beat)* See you then.

NICOLE: Bye.

GARRETT: Bye.

> *NICOLE exits. Beat.*

Holy shit.

> *GARRETT gets up to leave. A VOICE offstage calls out to him.*

VOICE: Hey Faggot!

> *GARRETT looks to where the voice came from and is greeted with laughter.*

See? Told ya he was queer.

> *GARRETT storms off frustrated.*

SCENE 5

IN FRONT OF THE SCHOOL

> *GARRETT, BRYAN and DIZ are hanging out in front of the school drinking Slurpees together. Bryan is in an athletic hoodie and Adidas pants.*

GARRETT: So, then she told me she wanted me to bring my decks tonight because she wanted me to show her how to play Magic.

BRYAN: You're shitting me.

GARRETT: No! Dude! I swear to God! That's what happened!

BRYAN: Right.

DIZ: Bullshit.

GARRETT: I'm serious!

DIZ: Why would she want to go out with you?

GARRETT: I don't know.

DIZ: I think it's a trick.

GARRETT: What?

DIZ: She's setting you up.

GARRETT: Why?

DIZ: Why? Why not? It's all those assholes ever do to us. Remember what they did to your car at the homecoming dance?

GARRETT: Diz, this is a little different than painting "faggot" on my jeep with shaving cream.

DIZ: How about that one time in the locker room after gym class? When the guys from the football team took your clothes and threw them in the girl's locker room? Then threw you in the girl's locker room in nothing but a towel? Then they took the towel and locked you in th—

GARRETT: I get the idea, Diz.

DIZ: Oh, and that one time when they jumped you in th—

GARRETT: Diz! I get your point!

DIZ: Sorry.

BRYAN: Jeez. Lighten up a bit. Not all jocks are like that.

DIZ: You're not a jock.

BRYAN: Varsity wrestling team? Varsity football team? Varsity baseball team?

GARRETT: Bitch, please. Haven's first titled assassin? Owner of the fastest NecroFurno Magic Deck in the school? How many Warhammer armies do you own, now? And I'm only counting the fully painted, combat-ready ones.

BRYAN *(beat, guiltily)*: Five.

DIZ: You're a closet geek.

BRYAN: I'm not a closet anything. They all know I game, and I don't get shit for it. You and I play Magic in the cafeteria every morning. It's not like I try to hide it.

GARRETT: So, you're a flaming gamer.

> GARRETT and BRYAN laugh.

BRYAN *(laughing)*: Fuck you.

DIZ: I can't believe you'd rather be labeled a jock than a geek.

BRYAN: Sorry if my strong sense of identity offends you.

GARRETT: Makes socializing easier.

DIZ: I still don't like it.

BRYAN: What? That I'm not waving the geek pride flag?

DIZ: Not you, dumbass. This cheerleader—

GARRETT: Nicole.

DIZ: Whatever. Garrett, you're not going, right? *(beat)* Right?

GARRETT: I don't know.

DIZ: What do you mean, you don't know?

GARRETT: I mean, I think this could be interesting. I want to see what happens.

DIZ: Garrett, they're going to trash you.

BRYAN: You don't know that.

DIZ: Yes I do! They're jocks! Fucking meatheads!

GARRETT: Diz, what's the worst they can do? Beat me up? I've got nothing to lose.

BRYAN: And the finest girl in school to gain.

DIZ: So, you're going to go?

GARRETT: Yeah.

BRYAN: What are you guys doing tonight?

GARRETT: Meeting at the movies at 8.

BRYAN: What are you going to see?

GARRETT: Who knows? I play my cards right and we won't even be watching it.

BRYAN: Whoa there, stud muffin. Seriously, you catch a cheerleader's attention for a minute and suddenly you think you're Don Juan.

GARRETT: Don't be hatin'. I just haven't busted out the Garrett charm in front of you guys yet.

BRYAN: What charm?

DIZ: Yeah. What charm?

GARRETT: What?

> *DIZ exits.*

What's gotten in to her?

BRYAN: Dunno.

SCENE 6

OUTSIDE THE MOVIES

GARRETT and NICOLE are walking to the movie theater. Nicole has changed into jeans and a sweatshirt.

NICOLE: So, yeah... cheerleading's ok, I guess.

GARRETT: Ok? Cheerleaders are like queens of the school, or something. How could that just be "ok"?

NICOLE: It sucks, really.

GARRETT: Bullshit.

NICOLE: I'm serious! When you're a cheerleader, everyone automatically thinks you're either a slut or an airhead and all of the jocks expect you to put out.

GARRETT: That does suck.

NICOLE: Yeah, most jocks don't like hearing "no" as an answer.

GARRETT: That goes for most guys in general, actually. *(beat)* What about Jesse?

NICOLE: Jesse... is a big jerk. We hooked up, of course, but we never did anything, y'know, major.

GARRETT: That's not how he tells it.

NICOLE: Oh? How would you know?

GARRETT: I'm friends with Bryan. Bryan sa— *(beat)* Never mind.

NICOLE: What did he say?

GARRETT: I really don't want to. It's no big deal.

NICOLE: No, I'm curious. What did Jesse say about me? And to who?

GARRETT: He says you guys slept together.

NICOLE: Ha. He wishes.

GARRETT: Well, what guy wouldn't?

NICOLE: I'm not going to answer that. *(beat)* Who'd he tell this to?

GARRETT: Well... Bryan...

NICOLE: He didn't tell the whole team, did he?

GARRETT: I don't know. Wasn't there.

NICOLE: Great. Everyone thinks I'm a slut that slept with the biggest bonehead in the school.

GARRETT: I don't think you're a slut.

NICOLE: I should transfer schools.

GARRETT: I'd miss you.

NICOLE: Huh?

GARRETT: If you left Piedmont. I'd, y'know, miss seeing you around.

NICOLE *(beat)*: What the hell kind of cheesy emotional crap is that?

GARRETT: My pathetic attempt at being sweet.

NICOLE: Alright, let me make one thing clear— you're not getting into my pants, ok?

GARRETT: I wasn't expecting to.

NICOLE: What?

GARRETT: I wasn't expecting to get into your pants.

NICOLE: Really.

GARRETT: Really.

NICOLE: So, what are you doing here?

GARRETT: You asked me out, *(beat)* and I didn't have anything better to do tonight.

NICOLE: Funny! What a funny guy you are!

GARRETT: Thank you. I try.

NICOLE: So, Mr. Funnyman, I've been sitting here telling you my entire life story for the past hour, but I don't know anything about you. What do you like to do?

GARRETT: Me? I'm a geek.

NICOLE: Meaning?

GARRETT: Meaning you wouldn't be interested in anything I do.

NICOLE: What? I'm not smart enough to enjoy your smart people games?

GARRETT: No... you're too... cool.

NICOLE: Cool?

GARRETT: Yeah. I mean, I don't get invited to parties with all the "cool people"... and this is my first date.

NICOLE: Ah ah ah! This isn't a date, remember?

GARRETT: Oh, yeah. Sorry. This is my first time hanging out with a girl.

NICOLE: Well, the parties are pretty lame, really. You're not missing much unless you like to drink yourself into a coma. Then, you wind up missing everything anyway.

GARRETT: You're far from the typical cheerleader.

NICOLE: Thank you. Nice dodge, by the way.

GARRETT: What?

NICOLE: Once again, you managed to avoid my question. You told me what you don't do. Now tell me what you do do. What do you do for fun?

GARRETT: Oh, y'know... the usual stuff.

NICOLE: No, I don't know. What's the usual stuff?

GARRETT: Oh... movies... video games...

NICOLE: Magic cards.

GARRETT: Magic. That's pretty much it.

NICOLE: You're lying.

GARRETT: Oh, c'mon! For Christ's sake!

NICOLE: No. What's your secret?

GARRETT: It's not a secret. It's... just a little embarrassing.

NICOLE: What, do you write sappy, angst-y poetry like the rest of the Goths?

GARRETT: I'm not a Goth.

NICOLE: You're not?

GARRETT: No. I'm a Geek. Goths're a little too "oh, pity me and my dark, sorrowful existence" for my taste. Good fashion sense, though.

NICOLE: Maybe that's why I got you guys confused. You all like to wear a lot of black. I mean, like a lot.

GARRETT: Yeah.

NICOLE: What's the deal with that?

GARRETT: Simplicity. Never hard to figure out what you're going to wear the next day.

NICOLE: Ever try any... color?

GARRETT *(beat)*: Why?

NICOLE: Never mind.

GARRETT: Ok.

NICOLE: You're good at this.

GARRETT: What?

NICOLE: Dodging.

GARRETT: What am I dodging, exactly?

NICOLE: Something I keep hearing you and your friends whisper about.

GARRETT: What?

NICOLE: What is "Haven"?

GARRETT: How do you know about that?

NICOLE: You and Bryan and that other chick—

GARRETT: Diz.

NICOLE: That's her name?

GARRETT: Her real name's Danielle.

NICOLE: How'd she become Diz?

GARRETT: Dizzy Devil was her favorite "Tiny Toon," so it kind of stuck.

NICOLE: Oh, ok. So, no more dodging! Haven. Yeah, so you guys talk about it, like, all the time. You really think no one's listening around you?

GARRETT: Seems like it.

NICOLE: Angsty. And you say you're not Goth. What is it?

GARRETT: Nothing.

NICOLE: You're certainly obsessed with "nothing," then.

GARRETT: Seriously, I don't think you'd like it.

NICOLE: Hey, I just want to know what all the hype's about. It's not like I'm going to ask you to show it to me or anything.

GARRETT: Ok... It's a LARP.

NICOLE: A what?

GARRETT: A game. Live Action Role Playing.

NICOLE: What's that?

GARRETT: You know the Renaissance Faire?

NICOLE: That thing where people dress up and walk around like it's the Dark Ages?

GARRETT: The Renaissance, actually, and yes.

NICOLE: Yeah, I've been there. I love their dresses.

GARRETT: Well you certainly have the... acreage... for the time period.

NICOLE: Huh?

GARRETT: Monty Python. Holy Grail. Y'know... "huge tracts of land"?

NICOLE: I don't follow.

GARRETT: It's ok.

NICOLE: You're not calling me fat, are you?

GARRETT: Oh, dear God no!

NICOLE: Ok, good.

GARRETT: Yeah, so Haven's kind of like a cross between the Renaissance Faire and your favorite action movie.

NICOLE: How does that work?

GARRETT: Well, Haven is set in medieval times. A bunch of people get together at a campground or a park or whatever land we can get and turn it into this fantasy world. You have a character and a costume and props and go on adventures. There's a team of people who run the game and tell the story and you get to play the heroes.

NICOLE: Sort of like make-believe.

GARRETT: Yeah, a little. *(beat)* I know, it sounds retarded but—

NICOLE: I think it sounds cool.

GARRETT: Seriously?

NICOLE: Yeah. When do you guys do it?

GARRETT: One weekend a month. Next game's in a week, actually.

NICOLE: Take me.

GARRETT: To Haven?

NICOLE: Yeah!

GARRETT: Hell no!

NICOLE: Why?

GARRETT: You won't like it.

NICOLE: Let me be the judge of that. I may surprise you.

GARRETT: Right.

NICOLE: I'm not kidding.

GARRETT: Sure you aren't.

NICOLE: I'm serious!

GARRETT: So am I.

NICOLE: I bet I can surprise you right now.

GARRETT: Whatev—

NICOLE *(interjecting)*: I like you.

GARRETT *(beat)*: Why?

NICOLE: Because you're the first guy that has ever talked to me without staring at my chest the whole time. We notice these things, y'know.

GARRETT: Really.

NICOLE: Yeah. There are other reasons, too, but that's a big one.

GARRETT: Wow.

NICOLE: You bring your Magic cards?

GARRETT: Yeah.

NICOLE: You still want to show me how to play?

GARRETT: Sure, but what about the mov—?

NICOLE: We can go to the movies next time.

GARRETT: Ok, co— wait, next time?

NICOLE: Yeah, if that's ok with you.

GARRETT *(beat)*: Sure.

SCENE 7

THE SCHOOL HALLS

GARRETT is recounting the events of his date with Nicole to an incredulous DIZ and BRYAN.

BRYAN: Bullshit.

GARRETT: I'm not lying, dude.

BRYAN: There's no fucking way she said she likes you!

GARRETT: There is and she did. What did I tell you about the Garrett charm?

DIZ: She's playing you.

GARRETT: Oh, for fuck's sake, not this again.

DIZ: She's just toying with you to get Jesse jealous.

GARRETT: It's ok, Diz. I know you don't understand what's going on here, but trust me, it's real.

DIZ: You think I don't know what it is to have a crush on someone and have them not see it? You're dumber than I thought.

BRYAN: We've all been there, Diz. Even me.

DIZ: Oh, thanks for the vote of sympathy, B.

BRYAN: That's what I'm here for.

DIZ: Great. Maybe you should consider a new purpose in life.

GARRETT: Ouch.

BRYAN: Hey, I was just trying to be supportive.

DIZ: I don't need your support.

BRYAN: Whatever.

DIZ: Whatever.

GARRETT: Whatever.

BRYAN and DIZ both look at GARRETT.

What? I just wanted to get in on the apathy.

They both look at each other. Beat.

What?

BRYAN: I still don't believe she said she likes you.

GARRETT: Believe what you will. It happened and it was incredible.

DIZ: Oh yeah? Then give us an instant replay.

GARRETT: Oh, right. How?

DIZ: You tell me. Here she comes.

NICOLE enters and goes to Garrett.

NICOLE: Hey! How are you? Listen, I was thinking. Can we get together to work on something for me to wear to the camp out? I wanted to come up with something special. Maybe you could swing by my place after I'm done with cheerleading practice? Sound like a plan? Good. See you at 5:30! *(turns to Bryan and Diz)* Oh, you must be Garrett's friends. I'm Nicole. Nice to meet you. *(Nicole waves)* Quiet bunch you are. Alright, I'll see you later. Bye!

> *NICOLE exits. Beat. BRYAN starts to clap and slowly ramps up into full blown applause.*

BRYAN: If I didn't see it myself with my own two eyes, I'd never have believed it. Well done, sir. Well done.

GARRETT: Thank you.

DIZ: What did she say about a camp out? You guys going camping together?

GARRETT: Oh. Um... yeah, we were, uh, I mean I was... going to bring her... next week.

DIZ: Next week.

GARRETT: Yeah... to Haven.

BRYAN: You're fucking kidding me, right?

DIZ: The fuck are you talking about?

GARRETT: She seemed genuinely interested in checking it out.

BRYAN: But Garrett, we're finally attacking the Dark One this weekend! We've been planning this for months!

DIZ: Garrett, that's our place too! You can't just invite her. You should have asked us.

GARRETT: I know, I know. I'm sorry.

DIZ: Uninvite her.

GARRETT: What?

DIZ: You heard me. She's not coming.

GARRETT: Diz, for Christ's sake, don't do this shit to me.

BRYAN: You're the one who did it. You shouldn't have invited her.

GARRETT: What's the harm in that? I mean, seriously.

BRYAN: You're the one who wanted the game to be a secret from everyone to begin with! You said that yourself! What the fuck are we supposed to do?

GARRETT *(beat)*: I can't just uninvite her.

DIZ: Yes you can.

GARRETT: It doesn't work like that. What's the harm in sharing it with her?

DIZ: She's a cheerleader.

GARRETT: So?

DIZ: So, we hate cheerleaders!

GARRETT: I don't hate this one.

BRYAN: I like everyone and even I think this is a bad idea.

GARRETT: Duly noted. She's coming.

BRYAN: Ok, well, then it's on you if your precious game gets fucked up.

GARRETT: It won't.

DIZ: Right.

GARRETT: It won't!

BRYAN: Ok, we'll give her a shot. (checks his watch) Ah, crap, I gotta get to practice. I'll see you guys later.

BRYAN exits.

GARRETT: So, you ok with things?

DIZ: No.

GARRETT: Why not?

DIZ: How could you go behind our backs like that? You want to date that slut, fine.

GARRETT: She's not a slut.

DIZ: Oh, so you're sticking up for her now, too? Garrett, she's going to ruin you. I just wish you could see that!

GARRETT: Diz, what do you have against me being happy?

DIZ: Nothing!

GARRETT: What is it then?

DIZ: Ugh! Never mind.

DIZ exits.

GARRETT: What did I just miss? Diz?

NICOLE reenters.

NICOLE: Hey!

GARRETT: Oh, hey...

NICOLE: Practice was canceled. You still want to help me make my character this afternoon?

GARRETT: Sure!

NICOLE: Great! Let me get my stuff. Be right back!

NICOLE exits. GARRETT watches her go. Suddenly, an apple core soars onstage and hits Garrett in the back of the head. Another VOICE catcalls.

VOICE: Hey queer bait! How much you paying her to cover you? She know you take it in the ass?

GARRETT storms off.

SCENE 8

THE WRESTLING ROOM

JESSE is working out by himself. DIZ enters. Jesse doesn't notice her. He continues to drill until Diz addresses him.

DIZ: Um, hi.

JESSE looks up, sees DIZ and goes right back to training. Looks intense.

JESSE: What do you want?

DIZ: It's not about what I want. It's about what you want.

JESSE: It's not you, if that's what you're thinking.

DIZ: I'm here about Nicole.

JESSE pauses.

JESSE: What about her?

DIZ: You want her back, right?

JESSE: No.

DIZ: Please. You still want her, and you want her to come crawling back to you because she dumped you and humiliated you in front of the whole school by dating Garrett. I know how you can get her back.

JESSE: Right, and why should I listen to you?

DIZ: Because Garrett's mine.

JESSE: Doesn't seem like it.

DIZ: That's because your bitch is in my way.

JESSE stops drilling and approaches DIZ, menacingly. Diz doesn't back down.

JESSE: Only I can call her that.

DIZ: And you wonder why she dumped you.

JESSE: What do you want to do?

DIZ: Ever heard of something called "Haven?"

SCENE 9

THE HAVEN CAMPGROUNDS

GARRETT enters in full battle dress. He addresses an army situated in the direction of the audience.

GARRETT: The time has come for the Free Army to take back what is rightfully theirs! For far too long, our peoples have lain scattered, like dust in the wind, under the oppressive boot of the Dark One's forces.

GARRETT (CONT'D): But now... now, we are united! Now, we stand here, together, on this field of battle today as one force! Today, the Citadel of Kabback-Bal shall rightfully return to the hands of the People! Are you with me?

> *Dozens of VOICES cheer back in reply.*

Good! You all know what you're supposed to do. Team leaders, report in. Everyone else, prepare for the assault.

> *NICOLE enters, looking stunning in a maiden's traveling dress.*

NICOLE: So, explain to me what's going on again?

GARRETT: A whole lot of fun.

NICOLE: Seriously? This is lame. It's two in the morning, I'm freezing and surrounded by a bunch of pear-shaped mouth-breathers.

GARRETT: That's not a nice thing to call Bryan.

NICOLE: Huh?

BRYAN: Behind you.

NICOLE: Jesus Christ! You scared the hell out of me!

GARRETT: That's his job.

BRYAN: Don't worry. If I'd wanted to kill you, you wouldn't have seen me at all.

NICOLE: Ok, Bryan, you're freaking me out.

GARRETT: His name is Sway here, Nicole.

BRYAN: Yeah, I'm just in character. I wouldn't really kill you.

NICOLE: You're a little scary sometimes, you know that, Bry?

GARRETT: Let's try to keep it in game, ok guys?

BRYAN: No prob, Ivan. *(to Nicole)* Well met, m'lady. I am called Sway the Silent.

NICOLE: You got that silent part, right.

BRYAN: May I have the pleasure of your name, m'lady?

NICOLE: Um... certainly, good... Sway. Um... oh, crap, Garrett, what's my name again?

GARRETT: Grizelda.

NICOLE: That name sucks!

GARRETT: Don't tell me! You picked it!

NICOLE: Well, I'm picking another one.

GARRETT: Suit yourself. Just don't forget to change your character sheet.

NICOLE *(to Bryan)*: I am Lady Amber.

BRYAN: Well met, Lady Amber. And what is it you do?

NICOLE *(looking to Garrett for help)*: Why, I... uh... I'm a Level 1 Elf Warrior! I smite things with my mighty blade!

> *NICOLE awkwardly brandishes a pathetic looking short sword.*

BRYAN: Very good! If only we had a whole army of fine soldiers such as yourself; we'd be able to... smite... the Dark One with no problems.

GARRETT *(aside to Bryan, serious)*: Methinks, good sir Sway, that thou had best silence thy tongue and be nice to the neo unless thou wishes to have my boot firmly planted up thine arse.

BRYAN *(beat)*: Very well. *(to Nicole)* Apologies, m'lady.

NICOLE: Apology accepted.

GARRETT: Weren't you supposed to give me a report?

BRYAN: They know you're coming.

GARRETT: Good.

NICOLE: Why's that good?

GARRETT: Because while I'm leading the team in from the front, Sway will be taking his crew through the back end of their camp and hitting the real target— their leader, the Dark One. We're just the distraction. It's almost time and we're all set except for...

> *DIZ enters, wearing her flowing sorceress robes.*

DIZ *(finishing his sentence)*: The artillery.

GARRETT: Indeed, Lady Mortania.

DIZ: We're in position, awaiting your command, Sir Ivan. Six Elementalists on the hill ready to rain fire and lightning on the battlements and two Necromancers in position to raise the dead back into the ranks.

NICOLE: Raise the dead?

GARRETT: We have a slightly different definition of "reinforcements" here.

NICOLE: What?

DIZ: Well, since we don't have any clerics that can resurrect characters in the heat of battle, we just raise them as zombies instead and throw 'em back into the meat grinder.

NICOLE: Ok, now I'm really starting to freak out here. This is still a game, right?

DIZ: Oh, no. We really do kill each other, then perform Satanic rights turning each other into zombies.

GARRETT: Diz! *(to Nicole)* Yeah, it is just a game. I know it sounds all weird, but it's going to be fun. Trust me.

DIZ: C'mon, Grizelda, can't take a joke?

NICOLE: It's Lady Amber.

DIZ: Oh, I'm sorry, "Amber."

GARRETT: Mortania, go get into position.

DIZ: I'm fine right here.

GARRETT: Now, Diz. You too, Sway.

DIZ: Whatever.

DIZ and BRYAN exit.

NICOLE: Your friends hate me.

GARRETT: I know. I'm sorry.

NICOLE: Did I do something wrong?

GARRETT: No, no. You didn't do anything. I fucked up.

NICOLE: How?

GARRETT *(beat)*: When I first brought Bryan and Diz to Haven, we agreed that this would be our place.

NICOLE: And you brought me.

GARRETT: Yeah.

NICOLE: I should go.

GARRETT: No!

NICOLE: Seriously, I don't want to get you in trouble with your friends.

GARRETT: You're not. It's ok. I'll deal with them.

NICOLE: I should still go.

GARRETT: Stick around just a little longer?

NICOLE: Why?

GARRETT: Because... I like you, too. This is special to me and I really want to share it with you.

NICOLE: Garrett, I—

GARRETT: You said you wanted to get to know me better.

NICOLE: Well, yeah, but I think I've seen enough. I'm gonna go.

GARRETT: Please, just stick around until sunrise? I'll take you back home myself.

NICOLE: ...Ok.

GARRETT: Cool! The fun's about to start, anyway.

NICOLE shoots him an incredulous look.

Trust me. Just watch. *(turns and faces front, addressing his troops)* On my signal! *(raises his sword)* Ready... CHARGE!

> *GARRETT slices the air downward with his sword. A chorus of battle cries rings out. The sound of charging feet is heard, then battle. Garrett watches with a pleased expression on his face. NICOLE moves up beside him, watching in awe.*

NICOLE: Whoa.

GARRETT: Yeah, no shit.

> *They watch the battle unfurl before them.*

NICOLE: That looks like fun.

GARRETT: You think?

NICOLE: Yeah.

GARRETT: You want to join in?

NICOLE: ...sure.

GARRETT: Ok. Follow me.

> *GARRETT raises up another yell and looks at NICOLE. She joins in, raising her sword into the air. They charge toward the edge of the stage as the lights cut to black.*

SCENE 10

HAVEN CAMPGROUNDS

NICOLE, BRYAN, GARRETT and DIZ are all sitting together wearing their Haven costumes and white headbands.

NICOLE: That was awesome!

GARRETT: Yep.

NICOLE: I mean, the guys with the strobe lights! And the fog machines! The door with the silly string and the fishing wire Bryan had to mess with and the two guys playing that... what was that thing?

GARRETT: A cave troll.

DIZ *(à la Sean Bean's Boromir in Fellowship of the Ring)*: "They have a cave troll."

NICOLE: Yeah... that thing was incredible!

BRYAN: You were pretty incredible yourself.

NICOLE: Me?

GARRETT: Yeah, I've never seen a neo fight like that.

NICOLE: You're just being nice.

BRYAN: No, even I have to admit you did well.

NICOLE: Really?

BRYAN: Yeah. I'm impressed. *(beat)* It's just a shame we all died.

GARRETT: That kinda sucked.

DIZ: I never knew you could do that with Exploding Runes!

GARRETT: Seriously!

BRYAN: That was bullshit!

NICOLE *(beat)*: So what happens to us now?

GARRETT: Well, first we get resurrected. Then we have to go back to the battlefield and get back our gear without getting killed again.

NICOLE: Really?

BRYAN: Yep. We'll have to be sneaky. I'm sure the Dark One will have guards posted.

NICOLE: Awesome.

DIZ: Just another exciting weekend at Haven.

NICOLE: You guys do this every month?!?

BRYAN: Yep.

NICOLE: Why haven't you told everyone else about this? This is fun!

BRYAN: I don't think everyone's nearly as open-minded as you are.

NICOLE: Have you even offered?

>   *DIZ, BRYAN and GARRETT all look at each other.*

DIZ: Not really.

NICOLE: Well, that's the problem right there. You guys should make flyers or something. A lot of people would like this!

>   *DIZ and BRYAN look to GARRETT. Beat.*

GARRETT: Um, well... Nicole, this is pretty special to us. We don't want just anyone coming here.

NICOLE: Why not?

DIZ: Because we hate everyone.

NICOLE: What?

GARRETT *(glaring at Diz)*: Because here, we're the cool kids. We don't want that to change.

NICOLE: Why would it? I can't think of a single good reas—

>   *A strobe light starts flashing.*

DIZ: Looks like it's time for the resurrection.

GARRETT: 'Least this time it didn't take three days, right?

NICOLE: What?

BRYAN: Catholic joke. Bad Catholic joke.

NICOLE: But what about—

GARRETT: We'll talk more about this later. If we want to rez, we need to go now.

> *DIZ and BRYAN exit. GARRETT starts to exit with them, but NICOLE holds him back. She kisses him tenderly, smiles and exits, following everyone else. He is stunned. Bryan re-enters.*

BRYAN: Fuck!

GARRETT *(exiting)*: C'mon, Sway! We gotta move!

BRYAN: I forgot my headband!

> *They leave.*

> *BRYAN quickly retrieves his headband just as JESSE runs on from the opposite side of stage. He's obviously trying to not be seen.*

Jesse?

> *JESSE knows he's been spotted. He runs back the way he came.*

What the fuck is he doing here?

GARRETT: Sway!

> *BRYAN exits after GARRETT, hesitantly.*

SCENE 11

HAVEN CAMPGROUNDS: COMBAT MONTAGE

This scene features several short "moments" that occur throughout the night's LARPing adventures. Entrances and exits should be lightning-fast, and the scene should be set to high-energy music played at a loud volume. Think "Sabotage" by The Beastie Boys. For the sake of the play, monsters and enemy combatants in this scene are all imaginary.

When the heroes fight, they shout damage calls with each swing of their weapon. GARRETT calls "4 Magic." BRYAN calls "4 Fire" with his Flame Sword, and "2 Ice" with his Ice Blade, which he wields in his off-hand. DIZ calls "3 Normal" with her staff, and also casts numerous spells, as noted below. Damage calls for special attacks are noted in the dialogue below.

NICOLE enters and charges across the stage, sword overhead, issuing a shrill battle cry. She exits the opposite side from which she entered. JESSE stumbles in from the same direction, clearly bewildered.

JESSE: Where the fuck am I?

> *He exits. GARRETT and BRYAN enter together, searching for enemies. They cross paths and exit at opposite corners. DIZ enters and moves center. She spies her foes.*

DIZ: Goblins. I fucking hate goblins.

> *DIZ engages her foes. In addition to her normal damage calls, she swings low on one opponent and calls "Critical Sweep!" On another, she swings her staff like a baseball bat and calls "Break Limb!" GARRETT and BRYAN enter. They move to Diz's flanks and engage more goblins, fighting valiantly. After a beat:*

Hey! HEY! GET BACK HERE MOTHERFUCKER!

> *DIZ breaks ranks and exits, chasing after her fleeing foe. GARRETT and BRYAN close ranks, now fighting back-to-back. They turn from offensive to defensive tactics, as the goblins start to overwhelm them. Their combat calls switch from damage to "Parry" and "Dodge" as they struggle to stay alive.*

GARRETT: Oh shit!

BRYAN: Where are they all coming from?

GARRETT: I have no fucking idea!

> *DIZ re-enters and plants herself firmly between Garrett and Bryan. She spins her staff in front of herself defensively.*

DIZ: By the Red Dragon, I summon a wall of fire!

> *GARRETT and BRYAN, heartened by the turning tide, strike down their foes, Garrett by bashing his foe with his shield and calling "Shield Stun!" Bryan shifts DSR.*

BRYAN: Ivan! Fire elemental!

> *GARRETT moves to BRYAN's side, and together they engage the new threat. Bryan drops his Flame Sword and fights only with his Ice Blade, putting him at a disadvantage.*

> *Behind them, JESSE enters. DIZ sees him and tries to get him to hide or leave before he's seen. He won't. She swings her staff at his head. He ducks, surprised. She chases him off stage, swinging at him wildly with her staff all the way. Working together, GARRETT and BRYAN finish off their enemies.*

GARRETT & BRYAN (*in unison*): Critical Slay!

> *They high five each other. BRYAN picks up his Flame Sword, then spies another monster offstage to fight.*

BRYAN: Fucker! C'mere!

> *BRYAN exits, chasing after his new target.*

> *Meanwhile, GARRETT quickly counts out the damage he took in his last fight and realizes he's nearly dead. He collapses to one knee. DIZ reenters and runs to his side.*

DIZ: By the Red Dragon, I cauterize wounds!

> *GARRETT is healed.*

GARRETT: Flame strike!

DIZ: By the Red Dragon, I grant you a flame strike!

> *GARRETT stands and the two strike hero poses as a new wave of enemies rolls up on them.*

Alright, bring it on, motherfuckers!

> *GARRETT and DIZ fight valiantly side-by-side. By virtue of the flame strike spell, their damage calls change to "6 Fire" and "5 Fire", respectively. After a beat, BRYAN enters USR and charges across the stage after another unseen target. He screams a battle cry all the way. All other action on stage stops as Garrett and Diz turn and watch him cross. Beat. They look at each other, turn, finish off their opponents, look back at each other, shrug, and with a battle cry, raise their weapons and dash off after Bryan. Beat. Diz, Bryan and Garrett run back on stage, making a hasty retreat and screaming in terror at whatever they just ran into off stage. They exit in the opposite direction. JESSE enters just in time to see them leave. Wondering what could have scared them, he moves towards the spot where they entered, looking offstage. Suddenly, he sees it.*

JESSE: WHAT THE FUCK IS THAT?!?

> *JESSE dashes off after Garrett, Diz and Bryan, fleeing in terror. Beat. DIZ re-enters from another direction and moves down center.*

DIZ: Alright assholes. Ten of you, and one of me? I got this. *(she raises her staff over her head)* ACTIVATE STAFF OF DESTRUCTION!! That's right, bitches! Shit just got real! *(she wields her staff like a magic wand, pointing it at her targets and incanting)* Incinerate! Incinerate! Incinerate! Shut the fuck up, Blake, you're dead! Incinerate!

> *BRYAN reenters. He engages a monster, deftly spinning behind it and delivering a fatal blow to its back.*

BRYAN: ASSASSINATE!

> *He moves to DIZ'S side.*

DIZ: Sway! Skeletons!

> *BRYAN shifts to engage the skeleton, dropping his Ice Blade, he wields his Flame Sword with two hands and takes a mighty swing, calling "10 MASSIVE!" He retrieves his Ice Blade.*

BRYAN *(pointing offstage)*: Cave troll!

DIZ: "They have a ca— "

BRYAN: No, seriously!

DIZ: Oh shit! *(beat)* C'mere!

> *BRYAN moves to DIZ's side. She spins him around so his back is to her.*

I've always wanted to do this. By the Red Dragon...

> *DIZ jumps onto BRYAN's back.*

I take elemental form!!

> *BRYAN roars. DIZ cackles with delight. The two raise their weapons and charge offstage, Diz riding on Bryan's back, as the lights fade to blackout.*

SCENE 12

THE SCHOOL HALLS

NICOLE is at her locker. JESSE enters.

JESSE: So, where you been?

NICOLE: None of your business.

JESSE: You were off in the woods with that freak and his friends.

NICOLE: How do you know about that?

JESSE: None of your business.

NICOLE: Are you spying on me?

JESSE: Nicole... I'm sorry. *(beat)* Look, let's just cut the bullshit. We both know you're leading Poindexter on just to get back at me. I'm sorry for messing around with Amy. She's sorry too. Can you forgive me?

NICOLE: No.

JESSE: Why not?

NICOLE: Jesse, to find forgiveness, first you have to feel bad for what you did wrong.

JESSE: I do!

NICOLE: No, you feel bad for getting caught. How long would it have gone on behind my back? How long was it going on for?

JESSE: Nicole, I made a mistake.

NICOLE: No, I made the mistake by dating you. Now, everything's fine.

JESSE: So, it's like that? You dump me and start sucking face with that faggot to get back at me?

NICOLE: Don't flatter yourself.

JESSE: Better than embarrassing myself. Everyone's wondering what happened to you.

GARRETT enters, carrying his notebook. He sees what's going on and goes to NICOLE.

GARRETT: Everything alright?

NICOLE hugs GARRETT.

NICOLE: Just fine.

NICOLE turns back to JESSE.

JESSE: You'll regret that.

GARRETT: Whatever.

JESSE: What was that?

GARRETT: Whatever, dude.

JESSE stares a hole through GARRETT.

JESSE: You'd better watch yourself.

JESSE leaves, purposely knocking into GARRETT as he goes.

GARRETT *(under his breath)*: Fucker. *(beat, then to Nicole)* What's up?

NICOLE: Nothing.

GARRETT: Doesn't look like "nothing."

NICOLE: It's ok. He was just being a jerk.

GARRETT: Well, if he starts any shit again, let me know. I'll bust out on him, Ivan-style.

Beat. NICOLE is unresponsive.

This would be a good time for you to swoon and go "oh, my hero!"

NICOLE: Oh, I'm sorry.

GARRETT: Forget it. *(beat)* Can I ask you an honest question?

NICOLE: Sure.

GARRETT: What's his problem with me?

NICOLE: What?

GARRETT: Jesse. What's his damage?

NICOLE: Why do you want to know?

GARRETT: Because I don't understand why people have a problem with me.

NICOLE: Well, I don't have a problem with you.

GARRETT: I know that. I mean the rest of the school.

NICOLE: I can't speak for the entire school, but I know Jesse doesn't like you because he sees how happy you make me.

GARRETT: Oh, really?

NICOLE: Yeah. He's jealous.

GARRETT: You're kidding.

NICOLE: Nope.

GARRETT: Do I make you happy?

NICOLE: What do you think?

GARRETT: You didn't answer my question.

NICOLE: Yes.

GARRETT: If that's the case, I think I can grow to like being Piedmont's Most Hated.

NICOLE: You've been different ever since we went to Haven.

GARRETT: You're getting to know the real me.

NICOLE: I like this "real" you. I wish I'd known about it sooner.

GARRETT: Well, I'm all yours, now.

NICOLE: Lucky me. *(beat)* You should let everyone see the real you.

GARRETT: Nah.

NICOLE: Why not? You've got nothing to be afraid of.

GARRETT: I'm not afraid. I take enough crap as it is based on what they think I am. Can you imagine what it would be like if they actually knew who I was?

NICOLE: What's wrong with that?

> *GARRETT looks like he's about to say something, but changes his mind at the last second. Instead...*

GARRETT: Nicole, I'm a geek. I'm not "cool." Why put myself out there when I'm just going to get rejected?

NICOLE: Well, I like to think I'm "cool," and I liked you a lot more after I got to know you.

GARRETT: You're kidding, right?

NICOLE: No.

GARRETT: Well, you're weird.

NICOLE: Yeah, but, I still am cool and I still like you, so we know it's possible.

GARRETT: It doesn't work like that.

NICOLE: Sure it does!

GARRETT: Not for guys like me.

NICOLE: Well, then just ride out the next two and a half years. Ignore it. I hear things only get better in college.

GARRETT: Gotta get there, first. It's a longer road then you think.

NICOLE: Garrett, what do you want me to say?

GARRETT: I don't know...

NICOLE: Well, if you don't like how people treat you, why not do something about it?

GARRETT: Oh, believe me, I've thought about it.

NICOLE: And...?

GARRETT: Promise you won't talk to anyone about this, ok?

NICOLE: I promise.

GARRETT: I don't know. Sometimes I get really angry and I start thinking that maybe the Columbine guys got it right. Y'know... make a grand statement, a big ol' "fuck you" to everyone that ever hurt them, and then go out in a blaze of glory.

NICOLE: Garrett, they killed lots of innocent people. They ruined the lives of their families and their entire community. The only thing they did was to make people afraid of people like...

GARRETT: Like what? Me?

NICOLE: Well, you and Diz and even Bryan are all a little "out there." You know... "on the edge." It's almost like you guys don't want to fit i—

GARRETT: We don't.

NICOLE: Well, be that as it ma—

GARRETT: People are afraid of me?

NICOLE: Yeah.

GARRETT: No shit.

> *NICOLE shakes her head.*

Damn.

NICOLE: Yeah. What, you didn't know?

GARRETT: I guess your definition of freak and mine are two different things.

NICOLE: Guess so. *(beat)* Garrett, you're not going to do anything crazy, are you?

GARRETT: Who, me? Nah... I know they were nuts. I can understand their anger, y'know, but I can't match their hate. They hated everyone.

NICOLE: But isn't that what you and Diz pride yourselves on? Hating everyone?

GARRETT: Diz does... but I don't. I like you.

NICOLE: Thank you. *(beat)* You're a good guy, you know that?

GARRETT: Don't let that get around. It would ruin my bad boy reputation.

> *They both laugh.*

NICOLE: So, what's with that notebook?

GARRETT: Hmm?

NICOLE: Is that for a class?

GARRETT: Uh... yeah. Geography.

NICOLE: You like geography?

GARRETT: Not really... why?

NICOLE: You carry it with you wherever you go at school.

GARRETT: Oh.

NICOLE: That's not geography.

GARRETT: It's my journal.

NICOLE: Oh. Cool.

GARRETT: Yeah.

NICOLE: Why'd you lie?

GARRETT: Honestly?

NICOLE: Um, yeah?

GARRETT: I'm embarrassed.

NICOLE: Ok.

GARRETT: Really?

NICOLE: Yeah.

GARRETT: Why?

NICOLE: I trust you.

GARRETT: Really.

NICOLE: Yeah.

GARRETT: Oh.

NICOLE: Shouldn't I?

GARRETT: Yeah, I guess you can.

NICOLE: You guess?

GARRETT: I mean, yeah, you can trust me.

NICOLE: Good. That's important. I don't want you to be like the last guy I couldn't trust.

GARRETT: Me neither.

NICOLE: 'Cause I burned him good!

They share another laugh.

GARRETT *(beat)*: So... are we still... um... "not dating."

NICOLE: Huh?

GARRETT: We've been to the movies. We've been camping. We've been out on a bunch of "non-dates" and have been seen making out all over school.

NICOLE: And...?

GARRETT: And I want to know... if I can call you my girlfriend.

NICOLE: Oh.

Beat.

GARRETT: It's no big deal.

NICOLE: It's ok.

GARRETT: It is?

NICOLE: Yeah.

GARRETT *(beat)*: Cool.

SCENE 13

THE CAFETERIA

DIZ is sitting at a cafeteria table, alone. She's rolled up her sleeve and shifted her cuff up her arm. For the first time, we see that the cuff had been concealing cuts on her forearm. She picks at them. BRYAN enters and heads for her table. Seeing him, Diz quickly pulls her sleeve down and composes herself.

BRYAN: Diz.

DIZ: Hey Bryan. Have a seat. What's up?

BRYAN: Nothing. What's up with you?

DIZ: Nothing.

BRYAN: I find that hard to believe.

DIZ: What makes you say that?

BRYAN: Saw you in the wrestling room talking to Jesse last week.

DIZ: Is that a crime?

BRYAN: Depends. What's going on?

DIZ: Nothing.

BRYAN: I'm not in the mood for games, Diz.

DIZ: I mean it. Nothing's going on. What's this all about?

BRYAN: I saw Jesse at Haven Saturday night.

DIZ: Bullshit.

BRYAN: He was hiding in the woods, watching us.

DIZ: Are you serious?

BRYAN: Yeah. I think he was there to fuck with us.

DIZ: I don't remember hearing about anything happening.

BRYAN: Well, that's because nothing did. But it's weird that they were there. It's like he was spying on us.

DIZ: Wow. What the fuck.

BRYAN: What I want to know is how Jesse found out about Haven.

DIZ *(beat):* You think I told him?

BRYAN: What were you talking to him about in the wrestling room last week?

DIZ: Stuff. Not Haven.

BRYAN: Diz, we've been friends for too long. Please don't do this.

DIZ: Do what? I didn't tell him anything!

BRYAN: Then what did you talk to him about?

DIZ: Nothing.

BRYAN: Diz, someone told him about Haven. It wasn't me. It sure as hell wasn't Garrett.

DIZ: Nicole.

BRYAN: What about her?

DIZ: I saw her talking to Jesse after Garrett invited her to the event.

BRYAN: About what?

DIZ: I don't know.

BRYAN: So what's the big deal?

DIZ: I don't trust her.

BRYAN: You think she told him.

DIZ: Yeah. Y'know... to rub it in his face... or whatever.

BRYAN: So why'd you go talk to him, then? I thought you hated everyone, especially jocks. Isn't that like walking right into the lion's den?

DIZ: That's none of your business.

BRYAN: What, do you have a crush on him or something?

DIZ doesn't say anything.

Oh. *(beat)* Okay...

DIZ: What? Nicole's the only one allowed to move up and down in this fucked up little caste system.

BRYAN: Caste system?

DIZ: I learned about it in Western Civ today.

BRYAN: Nice application.

DIZ: Thanks.

BRYAN: So... you were in the wrestling room the other day talking to Jesse about...

DIZ: A date.

BRYAN: Why? He's a dick. I'm his friend and I think that.

DIZ: I dunno... I always thought he was kinda cute... and with Nicole and Garrett and everything...

BRYAN: You thought you might have a shot. So, wha'd he say?

DIZ: Well, just like in the Middle Ages, the nobles are free to slum it with us peons, no matter how scandalous it may be, but the peons can't move up to their status.

BRYAN: So, he said "no."

DIZ: Yes, Bryan. He said no. He turned me down. Thanks for rubbing it in. Christ. I'm so embarrassed, I want to fucking kill myself. I need to think of a way to take some of these sneering fuckers with me.

BRYAN: You're starting to sound like Garrett.

DIZ: Well, maybe he's got the right idea.

BRYAN: No he doesn't.

DIZ: You have no idea what it's like for us.

BRYAN: Oh, cut the crap.

DIZ: No. You have no idea! Everyone likes you. Garrett and I only have each other. He gets me. We're... we're kindred spirits.

BRYAN: Now you're just being over-dramatic.

DIZ: Fuck you.

BRYAN: Diz...

DIZ: You done playing Sherlock Holmes?

BRYAN: Yeah.

DIZ: Good. Now leave me alone.

> *An uncomfortable silence settles.*

BRYAN: So, that's why you're sitting here all alone?

DIZ: I thought you said you were done.

> *Beat. BRYAN rises, frustrated, and exits. Beat. A FEMALE VOICE calls out to DIZ from offstage.*

FEMALE VOICE: Nice collar, freak!

> *DIZ doesn't respond, but we can tell it bothers her.*

SCENE 14

THE CAFETERIA: ANOTHER TABLE

> *GARRETT is sitting alone, eating quietly and writing in his notebook. BRYAN enters.*

GARRETT: So, what's with Diz?

BRYAN: Dunno.

GARRETT: Eh, it'll pass.

BRYAN: I dont know about that.

GARRETT: What makes you say so?

BRYAN: Something seems "off." This isn't the usual Diz depression.

GARRETT: She'll get over it. Anyway, so Nicole and I were talking and she thinks it would be a good idea for us to go on a quest for that chalice you were talking about before. Y'know, the one th—

BRYAN (interjecting): Don't trust her, dude.

GARRETT: I'm sorry?

BRYAN: Nicole. Don't trust her. She's giving me a bad vibe.

GARRETT: This is my girlfriend you're talking about.

BRYAN: She's playing you.

GARRETT: Christ, now you're starting to sound like Diz.

BRYAN: Well, maybe she's right. Woman's intuition or something. But Nicole's playing you.

GARRETT: What makes you say that?

BRYAN: Jesse was at Haven.

GARRETT: Bullshit.

BRYAN: I saw him myself. You calling me a liar?

GARRETT: No. But what's Nicole got to do with that?

BRYAN: She told him about it.

GARRETT: So what if she did?

BRYAN: He's Crispy. Totally über-Christian. They hate shit like Haven— think it's Satan worship or something.

GARRETT: Dude, she was having a blast. What makes you think she was trying to get Jesse to wreck the game?

BRYAN: I don't know. You?

GARRETT: Me?

BRYAN: Maybe Diz was right. Maybe this is just some big joke on you, dude.

GARRETT: Fuck off.

BRYAN: I don't want to see you get hurt, bro.

GARRETT: Don't "bro" me, bro. No one's putting one over on me.

BRYAN: I'm not saying they are. I'm saying that there's some fucked up shit going on here and I don't want to see anything happen to you.

GARRETT: So, what do you want me to do, O Great Caregiver.

BRYAN: Dump her.

GARRETT: Fuck no.

BRYAN: It's for your own good.

GARRETT: I'll determine that for myself, thank you.

BRYAN: I'm not kidding.

GARRETT: I know, and that's what freaks me out. Dude, this is the first time I've ever found something even slightly redeeming about high school. I have a beautiful cheerleader interested in me and she's a gamer! That shit doesn't happen in real life! Not to guys like me. Not ever. Don't fuck with this for me.

BRYAN: Garrett, you know I'm your friend. I have only your best interests at heart. For the love of God, dump her. She's no good.

GARRETT: You've lost it.

BRYAN: Take a look at how things are changing around here! You barely ever spend time with me and Diz anymore! When you do, you're either on the phone with Nicole or talking about her. Dude, we want the old you back.

GARRETT: So, that's what this is all about. You guys don't want to see me happy, do you?

BRYAN: It's not that at all. We see how much you care about her and how much you've put into this. She is going to hurt you.

GARRETT: Whatever dude. If me being happy here for once is such a problem for you, then fuck you and fuck Diz.

BRYAN: I'm just sayin' th—

GARRETT: What, are you jealous? That me, the geek, got the hottest chick in school over you? Mr. Social Butterfly? Mr. I'm-So-Fucking-Super-Cool-My-Shit-Don't-Stink-And-Everybody-Likes-Me?

BRYAN: Whatever, dude, that bitch has been around the bend so many times I wouldn't touch her with my ten foot coc—

> GARRETT stands up and grabs BRYAN's shirt collar, hauling him to his feet.

GARRETT: That is my girlfriend you're talking about, jackass. Say one more word about her and I'll blow your fucking head off. Do I make myself cl—

> BRYAN, having enough, reverses GARRETT's hold, picks him up by his collar and slams him onto the cafeteria table. Garrett is helpless.

BRYAN: Don't you ever do that again.

> BRYAN lets GARRETT go and starts to exit.

GARRETT: I'm serious.

BRYAN: Whatever dude. You're too much of a fucking pussy. Just put that in your little notebook.

> GARRETT gets up slowly and cleans himself off. He exits in the other direction.

SCENE 15

THE HAVEN CAMPGROUNDS

DIZ and NICOLE enter in costume. Diz is leading Nicole into the woods.

NICOLE: Where are we going?

DIZ: You'll see.

NICOLE *(beat)*: So, why didn't Bryan come this weekend?

DIZ: I don't know.

NICOLE *(beat)*: How long have you been doing this?

DIZ: I don't know.

NICOLE: Ok, so what do you know?

DIZ: What?

NICOLE: I'm just trying to make conversation.

DIZ: Well, I don't want to talk to you.

NICOLE: What's your problem?

DIZ: You.

NICOLE: What did I ever do to you?

DIZ: You don't remember?

NICOLE: Remember what?

DIZ: We used to be best friends.

NICOLE: What are you talking about?

DIZ: Y'know what? Fuck you.

NICOLE: Diz, I have no idea what you're talking about. I don't know yo—

DIZ: My name is Danielle, bitch. Danielle fucking Watts. You were my best friend in Mrs. Rooney's class.

NICOLE: Mrs. Rooney? She was my Second Grade teache—... Oh.

DIZ stares a hole through Nicole.

Oh, Jeez... Danny.

DIZ: Danielle.

NICOLE: We used to call you Danny.

DIZ: Yeah. Danny. When you started making fun of me.

NICOLE: When did I do that? I nev—

DIZ: You were my best friend. You, and Theresa and Alexis and Kelly. We were all friends. Then, my mom took me to get my hair cut one day and when I came in to school, you said I looked like a boy. You all used to call me "Danny the Man-y."

NICOLE: It was just a joke!

DIZ: I went home crying from school every day for the rest of the year because of your joke.

NICOLE: Sorry.

DIZ: My mom took me out of that school because of you. Now here we are again, back in the same school for TWO YEARS and you don't even remember me.

NICOLE: Danny, I'm sorr—

DIZ: It's Diz.

NICOLE: Diz, I'm sorry. Piedmont's a big place. I didn't even know. *(beat)* What can I do?

DIZ: Leave Garrett alone. Go away and don't ever come near us again.

NICOLE: No.

DIZ: That wasn't a request.

NICOLE: Why?

DIZ: You already took my friends away from me once. I won't let you do it again.

NICOLE: I'm not trying to take him away from yo—

DIZ: You don't even know him. You know that? You don't even know the first thing about him.

NICOLE: What's that supposed to mean?

DIZ: How old is he?

NICOLE: I dunno. 15? 16? So wh— ?

DIZ: He's 17.

NICOLE: How is he 17 and still a sophomore?

DIZ: Ask him. And then ask him why he got kicked out of his last school.

NICOLE *(beat)*: No. *(beat)* It doesn't matter. He'll tell me when he's ready.

DIZ: If you say so.

NICOLE: Is this why you brought me out here? This, and to rub it in my face how awful a person I am?

DIZ: No. This is.

> Two SHADOW MONSTERS, [BRYAN and JESSE, double-cast]
> dressed in all black with black hoods on, enter.

Have fun!

> DIZ exits.

NICOLE: What? What am I supposed to do?

The SHADOW MONSTERS surround Nicole and slowly creep towards her.

NICOLE (CONT'D): Oh, God...

GARRETT *(offstage)*: GET AWAY FROM HER!

> *GARRETT comes flying in, dressed in full Haven regalia and wielding his sword and shield. He slashes at one of the SHADOW MONSTERS as he charges past them to Nicole's side.*

NICOLE: Um... is this where I say, "My hero"?

GARRETT: Not yet.

NICOLE: What are they?

GARRETT: Shadows.

NICOLE: That's bad?

GARRETT: Very. I'm all out of mana. I can't cast a light spell. Do you have a light source?

NICOLE: No.

GARRETT: Well, ain't this a bag of dicks.

NICOLE: Colorful.

GARRETT: Hold tight. Let me try something.

> *GARRETT moves to engage the first SHADOW MONSTER. He swings at it. The Shadow Monster makes no effort to dodge.*

CRITICAL SLAY!

SHADOW MONSTER: No effect.

GARRETT: Fuck. Well, that didn't work.

> *The SHADOW MONSTERS touch GARRETT and NICOLE.*

SHADOW MONSTER: Paralyze!

> *GARRETT and NICOLE freeze.*

I drain your soul one. I drain your soul two. I drai—

DIZ *(offstage)*: By the Red Dragon, I summon a Fireball!

> *DIZ reemerges from offstage, chucking beanbags at the SHADOWS. She repeats the incant for each beanbag thrown. Her aim is true and both Shadows react to being hit by screaming their death throes as if they were truly being vaporized. They run offstage. Diz runs to GARRETT's side.*

By the Red Dragon, I release you. *(to Nicole)* By the Red Drag—... whatever. *(to Garrett)* You ok?

GARRETT *(quietly so that Nicole can't hear, seething)*: That was wrong.

DIZ: What part?

GARRETT: All of it.

DIZ: Oh? I'm sorry.

GARRETT: We'll talk about this later. *(beat, then, changing the subject:)* Wish Bryan was here; Sway could have taken care of those guys with the Flame Sword. That gives off enough light to banish Shadows.

DIZ: Shouldn't have pissed him off at school, then. Maybe he would have come. What did you say to him, anyway?

GARRETT: Nothing. You blew a lot of mana to cast all those spells. How are you goi—

> *JESSE enters.*

JESSE: Nicole!

NICOLE: Jesse?

GARRETT: What the hell?

DIZ: Are you in-game?

JESSE: What is wrong with you people?

GARRETT: You don't have to be here. This is our world. Go to hell.

JESSE: Your world? I live in the real world, freak.

GARRETT: Fuck off, asshole.

> *JESSE starts toward GARRET menacingly, but DIZ steps between them, giving Jesse the slightest head shake "no."*

JESSE: Whatever. C'mon Nikki. We're leaving.

NICOLE: No.

JESSE: Come on!

NICOLE: Garrett's right. I'm having fun here. Go to hell.

JESSE: I didn't ask.

> *JESSE grabs NICOLE by the wrist and starts to pull her offstage.*

This is for your own good!

NICOLE: Let go of me!

> *GARRETT charges JESSE and punches him in the face, breaking his hold on NICOLE, who runs to DIZ. Jesse is stunned for a moment, but then punches Garrett back, knocking him down. Jesse then jumps on top of Garrett and starts to beat him until Nicole and Diz pull him off.*

NICOLE & DIZ: Get off of him! Stop it! Help! Jesse, stop!!

JESSE: He fucking hit me first!

GARRETT is unconscious. JESSE grabs Garrett's discarded sword, breaks it over his knee and throws the pieces onto his unconscious form. NICOLE and DIZ are still huddled over Garrett. Jesse moves back into the darkness.

DIZ: You're fucking crazy!

NICOLE: Someone call an ambulance!

INTERMISSION

ACT II

SCENE 1
OUTSIDE GARRETT'S HOSPITAL ROOM

Lights up SL. BRYAN's in his street clothes sitting in a chair next to Garret's hospital room door. NICOLE enters, wearing a sweatshirt over her costume from Haven.

NICOLE: Where's Garrett? Is he alright?

BRYAN: He's asleep. They just finished patching him up. Your boyfriend broke his jaw in two places.

NICOLE: My boyfriend?

BRYAN: Yeah.

NICOLE: Garrett's my boyfriend.

BRYAN: Stop it. You know what I'm talking about.

NICOLE: What?

BRYAN: Haven't you done enough?

NICOLE: What are you talking about?

BRYAN: You told Jesse about Haven.

NICOLE: No I didn't.

BRYAN: Nicole, Jesse is— was, a friend of mine and I haven't even told him about Haven. Me, Diz, Garrett... we're the only three kids from Piedmont that play. No one else from our school even knew about it until Garrett brought you, and then suddenly your ex shows up and goes batshit crazy. Don't have to be a rocket scientist to figure out who did.

NICOLE: It wasn't me.

BRYAN: Bull.

NICOLE: I'm here to see Garrett.

BRYAN: He doesn't want to see you.

NICOLE: Whatever.

BRYAN: He doesn't. That's why I'm here.

NICOLE: You're lying. Get out of my way.

BRYAN: I'm not lying. He knows it was you.

NICOLE: What did you tell him?

BRYAN: Nothing.

NICOLE: What did you say to him?!?

BRYAN: Nothing!

NICOLE: Then get out of my way.

BRYAN: Not going to do that.

NICOLE: Why not?

BRYAN: Haven't we been through this before?

NICOLE: Bryan, I'm his girlfriend. I have a right to see him.

BRYAN: I'm his best friend. I'm looking out for him.

NICOLE: Let me through.

BRYAN: Are you enjoying this?

NICOLE: What?

BRYAN: The drama. Are you getting a kick out of this?

NICOLE: You're sick.

BRYAN: No, you're sick. I know what you've been up to. That you've been seeing Garrett just to piss off your ex.

NICOLE *(beat)*: No.

BRYAN: Don't even try to hide it. You think I don't hear things. We have a lot of the same friends, you and I.

NICOLE: Bryan, it's not what you thi—

BRYAN: Don't lie to me.

NICOLE: You don't understand!

BRYAN: Doesn't matter.

> *NICOLE tries to force her way past BRYAN. He blocks her way, but doesn't grab her.*

NICOLE: Bryan, get out of my way!

BRYAN: No!

> *She stops trying to get past him.*

NICOLE: I love him! You fucking asshole! I love him! Now let me go see him!

BRYAN: Does he know what you were telling people?

> *Beat. NICOLE slowly shakes her head "no."*

That he was a joke? That you were slumming it?

NICOLE: That's bullshit!

BRYAN: Go home.

NICOLE: No.

BRYAN: Nicole, I swear to Christ, if you hurt him again—

NICOLE: I didn't do anything! He's got nothing to be afraid of!

BRYAN: Nothing to be afraid of. Then why is my best friend's jaw wired shut?

*Crossfade to SR. In his hospital room, GARRETT is
unconscious in bed with a brace around his neck. He has a
black eye and his face is swollen from Jesse's beating. DIZ
sits next to him.*

DIZ: It's all my fault.

SCENE 2

GARRETT'S HOSPITAL ROOM

*DIZ sits beside GARRETT, choking back sobs as she rocks
back and forth. She goes to a charm hanging from one of her
necklaces and opens it, revealing a small razor blade. She
shifts her cuff on her forearm and begins a fresh cut. Before
she can get too far into it, Garrett stirs. She hastily re-sets her
cuff and conceals the razor before moving to Garrett.*

DIZ: It's ok. It's Diz.

*GARRETT tries to speak, but discovers that he can't. All that
comes out is a muffled moan.*

Don't speak. The doctors... had to re-set your jaw. They wired your mouth
shut. Here.

DIZ hands GARRETT a pen and pad of paper.

Use this.

Beat. GARRETT writes.

"What happened?" Um... well, Jesse showed up and grabbed Nicole. You
jumped on him... and... well... The cops showed up with the ambulance... and
when they found out what was going on, they shut the game down.

GARRETT writes "WTF?"

"W-T-F." Yeah, that about sums it up.

GARRETT writes.

Why'd they shut us down? Something about permits for weapons. Cops
found some of the real swords Blake keeps in his car. Staff got nailed for an
unattended campfire, too.

GARRETT writes.

"How long?" The doctors say your jaw's going to take 6 we—

GARRETT shakes his head.

What?

GARRETT writes.

Haven? How long will Haven be closed?

GARRETT nods.

DIZ (CONT'D): I don't know. They have to go to court and then file for permits. Could be months.

GARRETT writes.

"Nicole?" Don't know. She left with Jesse. *(beat)* I have to be honest. I don't think she's coming back.

GARRETT writes.

"Why?" Because... she's the one that caused all this. *(beat)* Garrett, who do you think told Jesse about the game? Where to find us?

GARRETT shakes his head, "no."

Garrett, I'm sorry. It's true. It's the only thing that makes sense. Nicole, Jesse... people like them look down at people like us. They're evil. Truly evil, for doing things like this to us. *(beat)* I'm sorry.

GARRETT writes.

"Hurts"? Here, push this button. Morphine drip. It'll fix everything.

GARRETT smiles. We see the wiring on his jaw for the first time. DIZ starts to cry. Garrett writes. Diz reads.

Nothing... I just... I'm sorry, Garrett.

GARRETT writes.

"For what?" That... that you got hurt.

GARRETT sits up and reaches out to comfort DIZ. She crumples into his awkward embrace.

Thanks.

SCENE 3

HOSPITAL HALLS

BRYAN is sitting in the hall. DIZ enters from Garrett's room.

BRYAN: How's he doing?

DIZ: He's ok. Sleeping again. Can't tell if the morphine's doing anything, though. He looks like he's still in pain.

BRYAN: They give him enough to share?

DIZ: No. Believe me, I asked.

BRYAN: Any idea how long he's got to stay here?

DIZ: I heard the doctors tell his mom they're keeping him a day or two for observation. He's got a pretty bad concussion.

BRYAN: Fuck... *(beat)* How are you?

DIZ: Tired. *(beat)* Any word on Haven?

BRYAN: Who knows? The game staff says that the police have closed them down pending completion of their "investigation" into our activities.

DIZ: Wait, Jesse's dad is a cop, right?

BRYAN: Yeah.

DIZ: Great, so, their "investigation" will be completed—

BRYAN: —never. Yeah, I know. It sucks. They're not going to do anything about Garrett, either. Jesse claimed self-defense, and they're not questioning it.

DIZ: Fucking bullshit.

BRYAN: Yeah, but what can we say?

DIZ: Garrett should have blown his fucking head off.

BRYAN: Diz.

DIZ: What?

BRYAN gives her a look. Beat.

That sucks about Haven. Garrett'll flip.

BRYAN: Yeah. What about you?

DIZ: Me?

BRYAN: I'm a part of Haven because I like the game, but you and Garrett both treat it like it's your religion.

DIZ: Nah, I'm only really into it because of you guys. You and Garrett. I'm sure we can find other stuff to do.

BRYAN: Really. I thought you guys were "spiritually connected."

DIZ: Kindred spirits.

BRYAN: But you're not hooked on Haven.

DIZ: Yeah. *(beat)* I'm worried about him.

BRYAN: Garrett's going to be fine. Even without the game.

DIZ: I know, but I can't believe what she did to him.

BRYAN: Who? Nicole?

DIZ: Yeah. That bitch.

BRYAN: You were right. She came to see him.

DIZ: She did? When?

BRYAN: About an hour ago. I did what you said. Told her Garrett didn't want to see her.

DIZ: Where is she?

BRYAN: I dunno. We argued and she left. She was pretty upset.

DIZ: She's got no right to be! Look what she did!

BRYAN: Diz, I don't feel right about this. Jesse hit Garrett, not Nicole.

DIZ: That bitch is responsible for all of this!

BRYAN: Okay, okay. Calm down.

DIZ: I will NOT calm down! She did this to him!

BRYAN: Diz, relax! You're going to get us thrown out of here!

DIZ: Okay... okay...

BRYAN: You ok?

DIZ: I'm alright.

BRYAN: Ok. *(beat)* Why don't you want Nicole to see hi—

DIZ: THIS IS ALL HER FAU—

> *BRYAN puts his hands over DIZ's mouth.*

BRYAN: Ok! Ok, whatever you say! Just calm down!

> *DIZ falls quiet beneath the muffle. Beat.*

If I let you go, are you going to yell again?

> *DIZ shakes her head, "no."*

Okay.

> *BRYAN uncovers DIZ's mouth.*

DIZ: Thanks.

BRYAN: No problem.

DIZ: You going to be back here tomorrow after school?

BRYAN: Nah, I got something I gotta do.

DIZ: Oh? What?

SCENE 4

THE WRESTLING ROOM

> *DIZ and BRYAN are still onstage together while the screen crossfades to the Wrestling Room background. JESSE enters the opposite side of the stage and starts the familiar warm-up.*

BRYAN: Nothing. Just tell Garrett I say "hi."

> *DIZ exits. BRYAN approaches JESSE.*

JESSE: You ready?

BRYAN: Yeah.

> *BRYAN and JESSE start to wrestle. Bryan is clearly far more aggressive and ruthless. He's not wrestling to win; he's trying to hurt Jesse. After a particular painful exchange:*

JESSE: Dude! What the fuck!

BRYAN: Pussy.

JESSE: Wha'd you say?

BRYAN: I called you a pussy, pussy. You gonna prove me wrong or am I gonna make you my bitch again?

JESSE stands up and gets in BRYAN's face.

JESSE: What's your fucking problem?

BRYAN: You, asshole.

JESSE: Why? Because I broke your butt-buddy's jaw? That faggot got what he deserved. Y'know what? I don't need to answer to you.

JESSE turns to leave.

BRYAN: You're gonna.

BRYAN grabs JESSE and spins him around. Jesse swings at Bryan. Bryan ducks and punches Jesse in the eye. Jesse crumbles.

JESSE: Way to stick up for your crazy little boyfriend, there, Bry.

BRYAN: The fuck do you know about him?

JESSE: More than you, apparently.

BRYAN: You don't know shit.

JESSE: We'll see.

SCENE 5

This scene takes place in three separate locations; two of them simultaneously.

NICOLE, carrying Garrett's school things, including the black notebook, is having a confrontation with JESSE in the school halls SR while DIZ still tends to a sleeping GARRETT at his bedside SL. UC is the hospital hallway.

NICOLE: You got what you deserved.

JESSE: Well, you should be thankful for what I did.

DIZ: How you feeling?

NICOLE: You broke his jaw!

DIZ: Does it still hurt?

JESSE: I was defending myself.

DIZ: There's always more morphine if you need it.

NICOLE: That's just sick.

DIZ: I know you're hurting right now, and not just physically.

JESSE: I did it because I care about you.

DIZ: I'm here for you.

NICOLE: You're a monster.

DIZ: I've always been here for you.

JESSE: I'm looking out for you. What'd he do?

DIZ: I always will be here for you.

NICOLE: He loved me.

DIZ: But you already know that.

JESSE: Do you know why he got kicked out of his last school?

DIZ: We're kindred spirits.

> *The lights fade down on Stage Left.*

NICOLE: Doesn't matter.

JESSE: You have no idea who you're dealing with. He's dangerous.

NICOLE: You're dangerous. Get out of my way.

JESSE: Where are you going?

NICOLE: I'm bringing him his homework.

> *NICOLE runs from JESSE. Lights down on Stage Right. She bolts from the school hall to the hospital hall. Lights up Stage Right. Nicole runs into Garrett's hospital room to find GARRETT waking up to DIZ kissing him. Nicole stops and stares in shock. After a beat, Nicole runs out, unseen by either of them. In her rushing, she drops Garrett's books. She reaches down to pick them up, and comes up with Garrett's journal. She's staring in horror at a particular page.*

Oh my God.

SCENE 6

THE SCHOOL HALLS

> *GARRETT's back at school. He spots NICOLE at her locker. He can't say anything, but he pulls out a folded-up note which he intends to give to her. Garrett approaches, but Nicole ignores him. Garrett offers her the paper.*

NICOLE: I gotta go.

> *GARRETT gently takes her arm and tries to get her to read his note.*

No. I need to go.

> *NICOLE exits as JESSE enters.*

JESSE: What are you doing?

> GARRETT stares at JESSE. Jesse sees the note in his hand and grabs it.

Leave her alone. *(Jesse tears up the note)* Now, you're going to listen to me. My dad told me what you did at your last school. I don't want to see you near Nikki again. If I do, I won't just break your jaw. I'll kill you.

> JESSE throws the pieces of the note in GARRETT's face and exits. After a tense moment, Garrett turns to his locker and opens it. We see inside on the projector screen; someone has hung a pink dildo upside down from the top shelf and posted a gay centerfold spread inside the locker door. Garrett's face has been cut out and placed over the model's. Another voice calls out at Garrett.

VOICE: Hey! Tough to suck dick with a broken jaw?

> Laughter. GARRETT is furious, but unable to speak. We hear what sounds like a low, guttural moan rise up from inside of him, but it's suppressed by his inability to open his mouth and release it.

SCENE 7

THE HOSPITAL WAITING ROOM

> BRYAN and DIZ sit in the waiting room. They're waiting for Garrett, who is getting his wires off.

BRYAN: This sure is taking a long time. How long did they say it would be?

DIZ: Only an hour or so.

BRYAN: Seems longer.

DIZ: What's got you so antsy?

BRYAN: What's the deal with you guys?

DIZ: Huh?

BRYAN: You and Garrett? What's going on?

DIZ: I dunno.

BRYAN: C'mon Diz.

DIZ: I'm serious. I don't know what's going on.

BRYAN: You two were making out! Well, as well as you could, considering the circumstances. How could you not know?

DIZ: How'd you hear about that?

BRYAN: What's the deal?

DIZ *(beat)*: Well, it's not like he could say "no."

BRYAN: True... that and he was pretty doped up. Maybe he thought you were Thora Birch or something.

DIZ: Oh, great! Just what I need to know!

BRYAN: I'm kidding. *(beat)* You really love him, don't you? Garrett, I mean.

DIZ: Yeah. Yeah, I do.

BRYAN: For how long?

DIZ: I don't know... a while.

BRYAN: So what about Jesse?

DIZ: What about him?

BRYAN: Did you really ask him out?

DIZ: Kinda. I mean, I don't know. I was jealous and thought it would be a good way to get back at him. Garrett.

BRYAN: And the whole thing about not telling Garrett Nicole was here to visit? Was that just a way to break them up?

DIZ: I don't want to talk about it.

BRYAN: Diz, what the fuck did you do? How deep does this go?

> *DIZ is silent. Beat. It all clicks.*

You told Jesse about Haven, didn't you?

> *DIZ doesn't move. Beat. Her silence gives BRYAN the validation he fears.*

What the fuck? This whole thing really was a setup, wasn't it? Except you're the one that set Garrett up, not Nicole. You're the one that got his jaw broken.

DIZ: I didn't mean for it to happen! IT WASN'T SUPPOSED TO BE THIS WAY! WHAT THE FUCK DO YOU WANT ME TO SAY?!?

> *It's BRYAN's turn to be silent. DIZ is sobbing.*

BRYAN: I can't believe this.

DIZ: I'm sorry.

BRYAN: Don't tell that to me. Tell that to the guy whose life you've made a living hell for the past two months. You owe him that much.

> *A cell phone rings. BRYAN picks it up.*

Shit, I need to take this. I'll be right back. *(exiting)* Hi, mom. Yeah, I'm still at the hospital.

> *BRYAN exits. A beat later, GARRETT enters.*

GARRETT: Hey! *(he sees Diz is crying and goes to her)* What's wrong?

DIZ: Nothing... I... I'm just glad you're ok again.

> *GARRETT hugs DIZ.*

GARRETT: Thanks. *(beat)* Where's Bryan?

DIZ *(beat):* He had to go.

GARRETT: Really?

DIZ: Yeah, he got a phone call from his mom.

GARRETT: Ah. *(beat)* Did... Nicole...?

DIZ: No.

GARRETT: Oh.

DIZ *(beat):* You ok?

GARRETT: Yeah.

DIZ: So, you want to go get some pizza or something? You haven't been able to eat regular food in weeks.

GARRETT: Sure.

>*They exit. A beat later, BRYAN reenters.*

BRYAN: So, did he come out? *(looks around)* Diz? *(beat)* Well, fuck. *(Bryan sits down to wait for Garrett and Diz, unaware that they've already left)* How much longer is this going to take?

SCENE 8

A PIZZA PARLOR

>*GARRETT and DIZ sit together. Garrett is eating his pizza with wild abandon. Diz hasn't touched her plate.*

GARRETT: Goddamn, I missed this. You never realize how much you want certain things in life until you can't have them anymore. Know what I mean?

DIZ: All too well.

GARRETT: We should call Bryan.

DIZ: Why?

GARRETT: Well, because... It's Bryan. Why not?

DIZ: He doesn't need to be around all the time.

GARRETT: What's going on?

DIZ: Nothing.

GARRETT: You haven't touched your plate.

DIZ: Oh. *(beat)* I'm not hungry.

GARRETT: Oh, hell, I'm sorry. We shouldn't have come here the—

DIZ: No, it's ok.

GARRETT: No, seriously, if you're not hungry, I could have gotten this to go.

DIZ: It's no big deal. I wanted some time just for us.

GARRETT: Oh. Ok.

DIZ: Yeah.

GARRETT: Well... that's cool.

DIZ: What do you think of me?

GARRETT: I'm sorry?

DIZ: Do you like me?

GARRETT: Of course I do! I love you!

DIZ: Really?

GARRETT: Yeah! You're like my baby sister.

DIZ: Oh...

GARRETT: What's wrong?

DIZ: Nothing.

GARRETT: Nice dodge.

DIZ: Huh?

GARRETT: Diz, don't bullshit me. What's wrong?

DIZ: Nothing! *(beat)* Everything! FUCK!

GARRETT: Talk to me.

DIZ: Don't you feel it?

GARRETT: What?

DIZ: The connection!

GARRETT: The connection.

DIZ: Yeah. The connection. Our connection.

GARRETT: I'm not following you.

DIZ: We shared something special!

GARRETT *(beat)***:** We did?

DIZ: That kiss!

GARRETT *(beat)***:** What are you talking about?

DIZ: When you were in the hospital. You kissed me back.

GARRETT stares at her blankly.

I was sitting by your bed while you were sleeping. I was talking to you. Telling you how I really feel... about you. About us. About what I really want us to be. I kissed you...

GARRETT: While I was sleeping.

DIZ: Yes!

GARRETT: I was sleeping, Diz.

DIZ: But you woke up! You woke up and kissed me back!

GARRETT: I did?

DIZ: Yes! Yes you fucking did!

GARRETT: I'm sorry.

DIZ: No...

GARRETT: No, Diz, I really am... I must have thought you were Thora Birch or something.

DIZ: Fuck you.

GARRETT: No, I don't mean that I would neve— fuck. No good way out of this, is there.

DIZ: Not really, no.

GARRETT: Diz, it's just that I wouldn't ever kiss you... like that. You're my best friend.

> *DIZ stares at him, a tear dribbling down one cheek.*

Look, I'm sorry you got the wrong idea when you kissed me while I was asleep and heavily medicated. I love you. Just not like that. Please don't look at me like that. I feel bad enough as it is.

DIZ: You feel bad?

GARRETT: Yeah! I do!

> *DIZ snorts.*

Seriously! I— *(beat)* Diz, what do you want from me?

DIZ: Doesn't matter.

GARRETT: Fine. *(Garrett gets up to leave)* You're not telling me something.

> *DIZ stares at him, saying nothing.*

Don't talk to me until you can stop bullshitting me.

> *GARRETT starts to leave.*

DIZ: Garrett. *(beat)* Sit down. I need to tell you something.

> *GARRETT doesn't move. Blackout.*

SCENE 9

THE SCHOOL HALLWAY

> *BRYAN is at his locker in the hallway. GARRETT enters, furious.*

GARRETT: You knew.

BRYAN: What?

GARRETT: You knew Diz lied to me!

BRYAN: Aw, fuck.

GARRETT: You didn't fucking tell me.

BRYAN: It's a long story.

GARRETT: How long? How long had you known?

BRYAN: When you got your wires off. In the waiting room. That's when I found out Diz had lied. I stepped out for a minute just before you were released. Came back and she's nowhere to be found.

GARRETT: That's fucked up.

BRYAN: Yeah, I sat there for another two hours before someone told me you two were long gone.

GARRETT: That's REALLY fucked up.

BRYAN: No shit. Haven't spoken to her since.

GARRETT: Can't blame you.

> DIZ enters, carrying GARRETT's trench coat. BRYAN and GARRETT eye her suspiciously.

DIZ: Hey.

GARRETT: Don't talk to me.

DIZ: I just wanted to say I'm so—

GARRETT: I said DON'T FUCKING TALK TO ME!

DIZ: Why?

> GARRETT pointedly ignores her.

Garrett... why? Why?!? It's not supposed to be like this. We're kindred sp—

GARRETT: No. No, we are not. I am nothing like you.

DIZ: That's not true.

> BRYAN interjects, defending his friend.

BRYAN: Are you retarded?

DIZ: I said I'm sorry.

BRYAN: Sorry doesn't fix shit! You lied to us and we trusted you.

DIZ *(to Garrett)*: But I love you.

BRYAN: Your love ruins lives.

> DIZ tries to offer GARRETT his coat.

DIZ: You left this—

BRYAN: Go away and don't ever come near him again. You understand me, you worthless piece of shit?

> DIZ backs out, trying to fight back tears. After a moment she exits, still carrying Garrett's coat. Beat.

BRYAN: You ok?

GARRETT: Yeah. *(beat)* No.

BRYAN: First time I've ever done anything like that.

GARRETT: First time for everything.

BRYAN: Dude, you want to talk?

GARRETT: The fuck do you care?

BRYAN: Hey, I'm your friend and I—

GARRETT: You what? You going to fight all my battles for me?

BRYAN: What?

GARRETT: You know what I mean.

BRYAN: No, I—

GARRETT: I can take care of myself.

BRYAN: Yeah? What are you going to get broken next?

GARRETT: I don't need your help.

BRYAN: Bullshit. Dude, you couldn't help yourself if you tried. Look where it got you last time.

GARRETT: FUCK YOU! YOU ARROGANT COCK!

> *GARRETT exits.*

BRYAN: Dude! I was just trying to help! *(beat)* What the fuck...

SCENE 10

OUTSIDE NICOLE'S HOUSE, THE SAME NIGHT

> *GARRETT enters and knocks on the door.*

NICOLE *(from inside)*: I got it, mom! *(Nicole appears in the doorway and sees Garrett)* What are you doing here?

GARRETT: You weren't at school today and you weren't answering your phone.

NICOLE: That's because I didn't want to ta—

GARRETT: I'm sorry.

NICOLE: What?

GARRETT: I know what happened. I'm sorry. I didn't know Bryan and Diz were trying to keep you away from me. I had no idea that was going on. I'm sorry.

> *NICOLE is silent.*

Diz was totally jealous of us. She told Jesse about Haven and tried to break us up. She told Bryan you told him and that's why he wouldn't let you see me in the hospital. They didn't even tell me you tried. I thought you'd abandoned me. Then, when I came back and you didn't speak to me, I thought... *(beat, taking her in)* Are you okay?

NICOLE: Leave.

GARRETT: What?!? No! Nicole! I didn't know!

NICOLE: I don't care.

GARRETT: Why? Nicole! I love you!

NICOLE: You lied.

GARRETT: How could I lie about something I had no idea what was go—

NICOLE: Shut up.

GARRETT: What the fuck is go—

NICOLE: This isn't a locker room. You are at my house and my family is home. Do NOT use that kind of language here.

GARRETT *(beat)*: I'm sorry.

NICOLE: I'm going to give you something and then you are going to leave. After that, you are never going to talk to me again. Do you understand?

GARRETT: No, I don't.

> *NICOLE glares at him*

Fine.

NICOLE: Maybe this will help. Wait here.

> *NICOLE goes back into the house, leaving GARRETT on the doorstep. After a moment, she returns with his notebook.*

Here.

GARRETT: Where'd you ge—

NICOLE: Your locker. I was bringing you your homework.

GARRETT: Did you— *(he looks at her and knows)* It's not what you think.

NICOLE: You promised you'd never lie to me.

GARRETT: I'm not.

NICOLE: You are. You said you weren't like them.

GARRETT: I'm not like them.

NICOLE: See, there's that lying again.

GARRETT: What lie? What am I lying about?

> *Indicating the notebook.*

NICOLE: Tell me what this is.

GARRETT: My journal.

NICOLE: The list of names?

GARRETT: Nothing... a joke. It's a stu—

NICOLE: A hit list?

> *It's GARRETT's turn to be silent. Beat.*

NICOLE (CONT'D): You have a hit list in there. *(beat)* Why are you a 17-year-old sophomore?

GARRETT: Huh?

NICOLE: Were you held back?

GARRETT: I don't know what yo—

NICOLE: I checked my yearbook. You weren't at Piedmont last year.

GARRETT: Yeah I was.

NICOLE: Not at the beginning of the year. When'd you transfer?

GARRETT *(beat)*: Third quarter.

NICOLE: Did we even have History together?

GARRETT *(beat)*: No.

NICOLE: So you lied.

GARRETT: Yeah. But that was before I knew the lying thing was a big deal.

NICOLE: Why'd you do that?

GARRETT: Because I didn't know you then. I just knew what I thought about you.

NICOLE: And what was that?

GARRETT: That a guy like me didn't mean shit to a girl like you. *(beat)* I wanted you to feel stupid. I was hoping you'd feel stupid for not noticing me.

NICOLE: Okay.

GARRETT: I'm sorry.

NICOLE: You've said that so many times tonight it's lost its meaning.

GARRETT: I don't know what else to say.

NICOLE: Why'd you transfer?

GARRETT: Honestly?

NICOLE: Of course.

GARRETT: I got expelled.

NICOLE: What for?

GARRETT *(beat)*: Bringing a gun to scho— .

NICOLE *(cutting him off)*: Get help, Garrett.

> *NICOLE moves to leave, but GARRETT stops her.*

GARRETT: No, you need to hear me out.

NICOLE: I've heard enough.

GARRETT: You don't understa—

NICOLE: Those are my friends!

GARRETT: What?

NICOLE: Those are my friends on that list! You freak! You want to kill all of my friends!

GARRETT: It's not like that.

NICOLE: Like hell!

GARRETT: You need to listen to me.

NICOLE: You need to talk to a shrink.

GARRETT: Why? I already know how to tell them what they want to hear.

NICOLE: We'll just see what the police have to sa—

GARRETT: No! Nicole, you're making a mistake!

NICOLE tries to leave again, but GARRETT grabs her arm.

NICOLE: Garrett, let me go or I'll scream. My parents are inside.

GARRETT: I will, but you need to hear me out.

NICOLE: Garrett—

GARRETT: Nicole, I'm the only guy in the world dumb enough to get caught trying to get a gun OUT of school.

NICOLE stops.

NICOLE: What?

GARRETT *(beat)*: I was going to do it. Shoot the place up. I got into school, past the metal detectors, past the rent-a-cops. It's a joke if you know how. I was in class. I asked for the hall pass and went to the bathroom, where I'd hidden it. I was all set to walk back in there and open up. Six bullets in the gun. I was gonna kneecap the first person that stood up, show everyone I meant business... so they didn't get in my way, then put four in him.

NICOLE: Who?

GARRETT: This guy. You know the type. He was a jock. Got his rocks off by torturing guys like me. His parents had money. He drove a Beamer to school. He used to beat the crap out of me every day. Stole my lunch. Threw my books all over the hall. Shoved me into the lockers. He broke my nose once. I was getting a drink from the water fountain and he slammed my face into the basin. Chipped two teeth, too. He got suspended for that. I thought that might have been the end of it, but it only got worse. He started to sucker punch me in the halls. Never in the face, though. Always in the ribs or the back. He was smart enough never to leave marks and he knew how to get me where it hurt.

Teachers were no help. They said I just needed to "ride it out." My mom told me that I was letting him get the better of me. That I shouldn't care too much. "Don't care," she'd say. "If you don't care, they'll stop bothering you." Whole lot of comfort when you're getting the shit stomped out of you. My dad never understood why I didn't fight back. I told him that I tried, but he just kept saying I needed to "toughen up" and "get 'em back." I didn't want any of it. I just wanted to get through it and be done.

GARRETT (CONT'D): I found Haven, and that became my reason for living. I found it a lot easier to get through the day knowing that I had something to get excited about one weekend a month. But he was still after me. I had found a way to "not care," but he was still after me. He must have known that he couldn't get to me as easily, because he kept kicking things up a notch. My locker got tagged. Went out after school one day and found the tires on my jeep slashed. Prank calls at home. Couldn't prove anything, but I knew it was him. All this time, I kept dreaming of ways to get him back. Beating the fuck out of him with a baseball bat. Hitting him with a taser. Slitting his throat. I just wanted to witness one moment in life where that stupid fucking shit-eating grin got wiped off his face. I just wanted to get the best of him once. I'd stopped telling my parents about what was going on. What were they going to do, anyway? I think they would have been too heartbroken if they knew how unhappy I was. I would rather let them be blissfully ignorant and think that finally, things were going well for me than know that they were raising a weak, pathetic excuse of a man for a son.

It was the winter dance. I had a date. I guess you can say I lied about that, too, but I don't really count that night. Quiet girl. Very conservative, but kinda cute. Bookish. I had a few classes with her. She must have regretted accepting my offer to go, because we danced together once before she ditched me to go be with her friends. I was all dressed up. My mom had bought me a brand new suit for the occasion. Dance was in the school gym. I headed into the guys locker room to take a leak at one point. I was just finishing up and there he was. He'd followed me in. He and three of his friends. I tried to leave, but they grabbed me. Tore my suit. A kick to the nuts and I was on the ground. And then... they all urinated on me. All over my face, my hair, my new suit. Like I was their own personal toilet. They just pissed all over me. When I got up, they laughed and shoved me back out into the gym. I don't know if anyone noticed me coming out. I left. Left my date there, too. I heard one of the guy's friends took her home that night. I drove home, and it was while I sat in my car on the street, waiting for the lights in my parents' bedroom to go out so I could sneak in, with the stench of his piss all over me and my new clothes, I decided I was going to kill him. Flash forward two months. I got the hall pass. Went to the bathroom. Got the gun... and couldn't do it. I sat in there for thirty minutes and couldn't do it. Bell rang and people started coming in, so I flushed the bullets and pocketed the gun. It was too big to flush. Instead of going to my next class, I tried to leave. I wasn't paying attention and set the metal detector off when I headed out the door. That's when I got caught. And expelled. And when I transferred to Piedmont.

NICOLE: I... I don't know what to...

GARRETT: Then don't.

NICOLE: I'm sorry.

GARRETT: I've heard that so many times in my life that it's lost its meaning.

NICOLE: But that was then. It's all behind you. Why...

GARRETT: Y'know, I thought that, too. But it's the same everywhere. Here, it's Jesse. Jesse, who beat the crap out of me every day. Jesse, who broke my jaw. And Diz, who ruined for me the only two things in my life I ever loved.

NICOLE: But you've got a fresh start.

GARRETT: No. I don't. I'm repeating sophomore year.

NICOLE: Garrett...

GARRETT: That's what I get for fighting back. I get stuck here longer.

NICOLE: You call that fighting back?

GARRETT: Don't judge me.

NICOLE: That's not what I meant.

GARRETT: I don't care what you meant. You wanted the truth. You got the truth.

NICOLE: Shooting someone isn't fighting back.

GARRETT: It is something. It's payback. It's justice.

NICOLE: It doesn't work like that. You're hurting a whole lot of people.

GARRETT: What about me? What about the pain they put me through?

NICOLE: You'd be hurting more than just the people that hurt you.

GARRETT: I wouldn't care.

NICOLE: How could you no—

GARRETT: I wouldn't be around for the aftermath.

> *NICOLE is puzzled.*

You're smarter than that.

NICOLE: You can't be serious.

GARRETT: It's the only way out.

NICOLE: It's a coward's way out.

GARRETT: Then maybe I'm a coward.

NICOLE: You're better than that. Garrett, *(beat)* I wouldn't love a coward.

> *She moves to embrace him, but GARRETT stops her.*

GARRETT *(beat)*: You really mean that.

NICOLE *(beat)*: Yeah.

GARRETT: So, are we still...?

NICOLE *(long pause)*: Garrett, you're a wonderful guy but you still need help.

GARRETT: So, no.

NICOLE: It's not like that.

GARRETT: I don't need your pity.

NICOLE: What?

GARRETT: You told me to never speak to you again. Fine. You've got your wish. And now you know all of my dirty little secrets, too. Have fun telling all your friends about what the freak's really like, cheerleader.

> *GARRETT turns and starts to leave.*

NICOLE: Garrett!

GARRETT: What!

NICOLE: Things can get better.

GARRETT: Not for me.

> *GARRETT exits.*

NICOLE: Garrett!

SCENE 11

THE WRESTLING ROOM

> *On lights up, we discover GARRETT standing in the doorway, expressionless. The door is closed behind him. His hands are tucked into the pockets of his hoodie. BRYAN is leaning against the wall in his sweats. JESSE notices Garrett, and stops practicing.*

JESSE: Well, well, well. If it isn't the Fag in the Iron Mask. Where's your sword?

GARRETT: Fuck off, cockbag.

JESSE: What did you just call me?

BRYAN: Garrett, what are you doing?

GARRETT: I called you a cockbag. Are you too deaf to hear me or just too fucking stupid to understand?

JESSE: You want me to break your jaw again?

GARRETT: Bring it on.

> *GARRETT and JESSE start to go for each other, but BRYAN intercepts Garrett and takes him across the room.*

BRYAN: Think about this. He's going to kill you.

GARRETT: I know what I'm doing.

BRYAN: Keep talking like that and he's going to fuck you up even worse than before.

GARRETT (*quietly to Bryan, sarcastic*): That's why you're here. If I'm in trouble, I'll need you to pull him off me.

BRYAN: You're crazy.

GARRETT: Let me do this.

> *Beat. BRYAN lets GARRETT go. Garrett and JESSE square off center stage. To Jesse:*

You don't scare me. I've lived in fear of you for a long time now, but you don't scare me anymore. You think you can just push me around? You think you can do what you want to me? Try it again, and I guarantee I will do it right back to you.

JESSE: Whatever, fag.

> *JESSE pushes GARRETT. Garrett finally takes his hands out of his pockets... and, empty-handed, pushes Jesse right back.*

GARRETT: C'mon.

> *JESSE pushes GARRETT again. Garrett pushes right back.*

JESSE: I'm going to break you again.

GARRETT: I'll break you right back.

> *JESSE grabs GARRETT's collar and gets ready to punch him. Garrett, unflinchingly grabs the front of Jesse's singlet and cocks back a fist of his own.*

GARRETT (CONT'D): I don't care if you ever like me, but you will fucking respect me.

> *Beat. A faint popping noise can be heard in the hall. The sound grows louder, along with the sounds of screaming and people running.*

BRYAN: What the fuck?

JESSE: What's goin' on?

GARRETT: Don't know. Sounds like fireworks.

> *The TRIO head to the doorway. Before they can reach it, they hear:*

NICOLE (*offstage*): What do you want?

> *Gunshots. The boys stop dead in their tracks. Beat.*
>
> *DIZ enters, clad in Garrett's trench coat. One of the sleeves is rolled up, revealing a series of vicious-looking self-inflicted cuts running up her arm. They bleed freely.*

GARRETT: Diz?

> *DIZ raises a handgun previously concealed by the long coat sleeves and levels it at GARRETT.*

GARRETT (CONT'D): What the fuck are you doing?

A gunshot rings out and GARRETT hits the floor, clutching his chest. BRYAN and JESSE stand, shocked and dumbfounded. Everything is happening too quickly for them to react. DIZ aims and shoots both of them in cold blood. She then moves center stage. Tears are streaming down her face. She holds the gun to her head and pulls the trigger. It clicks, empty. Beat. Blackout. We hear the sounds of quiet sobbing and a new clip being loaded. Moments later, a final gunshot rings out. Silence.

EPILOGUE

*Two beats after the final gunshot rings out, the speakers
come to life again in the blackout. The first news report is
played again, this time in its entirety.*

REPORTER #1: Another tragic school shooting rocked the nation today. Barely
a year after the massacre at Columbine High School in Littleton, Colorado,
the bodies of almost a dozen students and faculty from our own Piedmont
High School were removed after a brutal rampage that was over before
many knew anything had happened. The violence started in the hallways
before spilling into the crowded Athletics room. The shooter, now identified
as Sophomore Danielle Watts, 15, fired indiscriminately into crowds of
fleeing students, before reportedly taking her own life. This horrific incident
of teen violence leaves a community reeling and families asking, "why?" Will
we ever know the answer? More on this story at 6. In other news...

PROPERTY LIST

- 5 Boffer (LARP-safe) swords and other assorted hand weapons*
- 8 LARP-safe Spell Packets*
- 2 Magic: The Gathering decks
- 3 Slurpees
- Composition Notebook
- 2 Backpacks
- 4 White Headbands
- Pencil & Paper (or mini whiteboard & marker)
- Cell phone
- 2 slices of pizza on paper plates
- Blank-firing pistol or prop gun

*Instructions on how to build your own LARP-safe swords and Spell Packets can be found at www.friendsliketheseplay.com.

Additional Titles From Stage Rights

The Jungle Book by Briandaniel Oglesby

"**Four Stars. An entertaining family show, with enough clever jokes to keep the grownups on board.**" –*Sacramento News and Review*

Mowgli's search for home takes the spotlight in this modern look at the classic tale.

Drama | 5F, 6M, Ensemble | 75 minutes

The Snow Queen

Book by Kirsten Brandt & Rick Lombardo | Music by Haddon Kime | Lyrics by Kirsten Brandt, Haddon Kime & Rick Lombardo | Additional Music by Rick Lombardo

"**A fairy-tale that rocks!**" –*The New York Times*

Urban steampunk and a pop-rock score amp up the Hans Christian Andersen classic that inspired the hit Disney movie *Frozen*.

Musical | 5F, 4M, Ensemble | 2 hours

Princess K.I.M.: The Musical

Created by Maryann Cocca-Leffler | Adapted by Maryann Cocca-Leffler & Toby Tarnow | Lyrics by Andrew Cass | Music by Andrew Cass & Premik Russell Tubbs

"**Our community fell in love with Princess K.I.M.!**" –*Monica Nadon, Director, TCT Community Players*

The popular children's books come to life onstage in this award-winning musical.

Musical | 11F, 5M, Ensemble | 110 Minutes

Christmas Is Here Again

Book, Music, & Lyrics by Brad Carroll & Jeremy Mann

"**The magic of the season comes alive!**" –*Santa Maria Sun*

Based on the award-winning animated film! Follow the adventures of Sophiana as she tries to win back Santa's enchanted toy sack.

Family Holiday Musical | 3F, 6M, Ensemble | 1 hour 50 minutes

Additional Titles From Stage Rights

Searching For Romeo

Book, Music, and Lyrics by Brian Sutton

"A refreshing take on Shakespeare and the modern musical." –*Broadway Spotted*

A retro-pop musical twist on the beloved Shakespeare classic *Romeo & Juliet* set in a modern day high school.

Musical | 7F, 8M, Ensemble | 1 hour 45 minutes

Gary Goldfarb: Master Escapist

Book & Lyrics by Omri Schein
Music by James Olmstead

"Bliss and a half— tremendous fun!" –*The New York Times*

Experience the magic of Gary Goldfarb as he re-creates Houdini's most dangerous escape to win over the girl of his dreams.

Musical | 3F, 3M | 1 hour, 35 minutes

Camp Rolling Hills

Book and Lyrics by David Spiegel & Stacy Davidowitz
Music and Lyrics by Adam Spiegel

Relive the days of lanyards, bunk beds and bug juice!

Whether you play sports or pranks, at *Camp Rolling Hills,* it doesn't matter if you're a bookworm, jock, or girly-girl because true friendships are made when all the rules are broken.

Musical | 8F, 8M | 1 hour 45 minutes

Up To You!

Book & Music by Eric Rockwell
Lyrics by Joanne Bogart

"Wry, witty, and ultimately courageous." –*New York Times*

Mean Girls meets *High School Musical* when Hamilton High is rocked by a political scandal.

Musical | 12F, 12M, Ensemble | 60 minutes

STEELE SPRING
STAGE RIGHTS

Made in the USA
Charleston, SC
29 March 2016